STOP SELLING
and
GET CLIENTS

The 9 Proven Steps for Professionals,
who want More Clients,
(without even selling)

By Bernie De Souza

THIS BOOK IS FOR YOU IF...

* You are technically at the top of your game but are struggling to get more clients.

* You know you should be earning more money but are struggling to get there.

* You want more top-quality referrals and personal introductions but are not sure how to get them.

* You would like a diary full of appointments but do not know what to say on the phone.

* You feel clumsy at networking events because you have not had training in this area.

* You feel frustrated when trying to close or complete new business and it takes too long.

* You would like to build instant trust but are not really sure how to do this.

* You would like to be more focused but get easily distracted.

* You would like more clients without the stress of selling.

* You want to know the exact words to use when presenting in public.

DEDICATION

I dedicate this book …

To my four children: Luke, Josh, Danny and Emma.

To my mother, who encouraged me to dream big from an early age.

I thank you all.

APPRECIATION

I am indebted to Tom "Big Al Schreiter" for the final format of this book. He has, single-handedly, been my inspiration, source of wisdom and friend over the last few years teaching me the real secrets of getting clients. I must note his help with the first chapter of this book, based on his own book, *How to Get Instant Trust, Belief, Influence and Rapport! 13 Ways to Create Open Minds By Talking to The Subconscious Mind.*

Thanks a million, Tom.

ACKNOWLEDGEMENTS

Many people have helped me in different ways throughout my working life and I thank you all for your inputs and encouragement to bring this book to completion.

To Peter Thomson: For his product creation programme and help with polishing the 15 Magic Words programme by using tips from his agenda and the Secret Grid.

To Dr. Robert Rohm: For the training in personality profiling.

To Carl Smith: For support and help and being the link between myself and Dr. Robert Rohm.

To Joe & Dawn Picci: For the help on sales training and giving me the confidence to go from MLM to corporate training.

To Graham Giager: For showing me how to solve problems quickly and also the art of delegation and getting things done quickly and efficiently.

To Sean Mckillop: For introducing me to other business partners and promoting the skills that I teach.

To Peter Edwards: For giving me the opportunity to help a FTSE 100 company train their advisors.

To Matt Payne: For promoting me to others in his organisation of 2,000 advisors.

To Pete Folan: For giving me the opportunity to train his team and for promoting me to train the UK advisors.

To Kevin Mitchell: For being a trusted friend and advisor with all my legal work.

To Robin Broughton: For his leadership training and being the friend who had the idea for the title of this book.

To Keith Richards: For instructing me to speak and train the Personal Finance Society in the UK. As the CEO of 122,000 members, his confidence in the programme was the key to my being able to help his members.

To John McGiven: for his friendship and spiritual wisdom.

To David Cook: my great friend for over twenty years, the backbone of this work. He has taken my notes, transcripts, telephone calls and vision and patiently helped me piece together the ideas in this book.

FOREWORD

The nine steps described in this book are the result of personal and business experience that Bernie De Souza has gained throughout his working life.

It clearly and logically takes the professional step by step through the process of establishing business relationships with new clients. As these steps are practiced and developed to become habits they will help the individual to achieve more and be more (without even selling.) These steps are not loose theories but are tried and tested techniques that both Bernie and others have proven work in their lives to make real and profound changes.

We hope you will enjoy the book and take on-board the information but most importantly, put it into action. We wish you every success in achieving your goals.

- Allan & Barbara Pease

Best-selling authors and motivational speakers

www.peasetraining.com

CONTENTS

INTRODUCTION

My sales career started 22 years ago with mobile phones. I joined a sales training course and became technically equipped with data about all the features available such as weight, size, coverage, functions, etc.

I was more knowledgeable about the product than anyone else on the course of 20 sales reps. However, after the course, I did not sell any phones during my first 90 days.

It was the Friday afternoon before the completion of my 3-month trial period when the sales director asked me to come back on Monday at lunchtime with my car and all my company belongings. His parting words were: "Have a great weekend." That weekend marked a changing point in my sales career and my life.

My wife told me she was pregnant with our first baby. I had to decide what to do. Should I accept the sack, and then look for a safe job and live a very ordinary life? Or should I learn how to engage with people and to sell and present?

During that weekend I found out about a course in Canada, costing £5000. I borrowed money from my friends and family, put the money into the bank on Monday morning and then paid for the course. At lunchtime, I went to the meeting expecting to be fired. I explained to the boss that if he fired me I would work for a competitor with the new skills I would learn in my training the following weekend. He gave me another 90-day trial period. I learned some incredible skills in Canada.

The most valuable thing I learned during that weekend was what Albert E.N. Gray had defined as "the common denominator of success." In 1940, he interviewed the top 100 self-made millionaires in the world and he came up with this statement after several years' research:

"The common denominator of success --- the secret of success of every man who has ever been successful --- lies in the fact that he formed the habit of doing things that failures don't like to do."

The four main groups of habits I learned that weekend were:

1. Prospecting habits (how to use the phone to get appointments)

2. Calling habits (making presentations)

3. Selling habits

4. Working habits (time management and how to use your diary)

That weekend changed my life forever. 90 days after attending the course, I sold 60 phones and made £60,000.

I decided to set up a training company and teach these groups of habits. I have never looked back.

My good friend, Tom "Big Al" Schreiter, wrote the book, *How To Get Instant Trust, Belief, Influence And Rapport! 13 Ways To Create Open Minds By Talking To The Subconscious Mind.* This book is the simplest explanation I know of on how to build trust instantly with clients. With Tom's permission, I customized his methods for Professional Advisors. These examples should make it easy for you to create that strong, friendly bond with your potential and present clients.

In this book I refer to people as "he" or "she" but the words are interchangeable.

"Make a friend by being a friend."

~ Ralph Waldo Emerson ~

1. The Secret to Building Instant Trust in Seconds

1.1 When You Meet a Prospect

Your prospective client sets an appointment for their initial consultation with you. Nervous, they arrive at your office, sit down, and begin to explain their problem.

Now, this prospective client can describe his problem to many different Professional Advisors, but the problem remains the same. So why does this person choose you? Or rather, how do they decide to not choose one of the other firms? It could be any number of reasons such as the following:

* Your academic credentials.

* Your communications appeared to be honest.

* The size of your office.

* The free coffee was tasty.

* The chairs were soft.

* The testimonials on your website.

* The pictures on your wall.

* Your suit appeared expensive.

* Your commanding voice.

1

* The courtesy of reception.

* The graphics of your ad.

* Your all-knowing nodding when they talk.

* Your description of your fees.

* The payment plan.

* It is just possible that a friend recommended him to choose you.

Having selected you, your prospective client arrives for your first meeting. In a very short time he will make up his mind whether or not to trust and believe you. This is the first impression even before you make any presentation. The prospect decides whether or not to accept that what you say is true. More often than not the prospect will not change from that decision.

Similarly you, the Professional, also make up your mind that you have made the sale even before you start your presentation. Building trust and belief with prospects within seconds is done by speaking directly to their core values, their subconscious minds. It's quite simple. Very quickly you develop a vocabulary of simple phrases and techniques to communicate that you are trustworthy.

However trustworthy you may be, unless you understand how prospects make their final decision, you will continue to miss potential business and fees.

Consider first the criteria that potential clients use to choose who should represent them.

The major hurdle for you to overcome is to guide your prospect to the belief that what you tell him in your presentation is true. Before Professionals start their presentation they create trust and belief in the prospect.

Before the client begins to describe his problem, he has a sense whether or not there is immediate trust - or distance - between the two of you. He wants assurance that you understand and see the world, and his problem, from his viewpoint. If he feels that you see his issues from a different point of view, he will be sceptical for the rest of your meeting.

You may be filled with sincerity and integrity, you may be honest and your product may be the best there is, but without trust the prospect will not listen to you with belief.

A good example of trust is when the leader of a political party speaks. If you are a member of that party, you naturally trust him and accept what the leader says as true. The leader has the same political viewpoint as you. If you are a member of a different political party, then you will not trust him and you will be sceptical. You will reject whatever the speaker says, simply because you have a different viewpoint; you see politics and the world quite differently from him.

And what happens when your potential client doesn't feel trust during your first meeting?

The potential client is unlikely to say, "I don't think you and I can work together, we just don't connect." Instead, he will delay the process by saying something like:

* "I need to get back to you."

* "I need to think about it."

* "I will talk it over with my partner."

* "I will make a decision soon …"

Then he will find a competing professional advisor that he can "connect" with and feel secure.

Unless you develop trust with your prospect he will put forward any number of objections, you might call them excuses, to your proposal; typical ones such as:

* "I can't afford it."

* "I will not decide now, I need time."

* "This isn't for me."

* "I'm too busy."

It doesn't matter what the reason (or excuse) is, if the prospect doesn't believe you, if you haven't built trust with him, he will give you any reason for not going along with your idea or doing business with you. This is not the time for you to practice handling objections because they would not have arisen if your prospect had trusted you in the first place. Once your prospect trusts you he will be happy to do business with you.

So how do we let our potential client know that we share his point of view?

We tell him one or two facts in life that you and he both believe to be true. The list below gives some examples that you could develop and relate to the particular client and meeting:

"Everybody knows that life insurance can be expensive."

"It is hard to live today and still have enough money to save for the future."

"Nobody buys risky investments with their hard-earned savings."

"It is hard to become an expert on tax strategies for retirement."

"We all want to know more options before we set a strategy."

"Most people find professional advisors intimidating."

"Some people think they can't afford professional advice."

"Most people have no relationship with their professional advisor."

"Smart people worry about their retirement."

"Most people think they aren't rich enough to have an advisor."

Very soon your potential client realizes that you are on his side and share his opinions, you share the same viewpoints. Now your client can set aside his fears, scepticism, disbelief and stress, and feel that, at last, he has found someone who understands his problem and is able to help him to resolve it.

Even before the issue is described, your potential client trusts you sufficiently to make the first step towards you in his selection process. With instant trust, your prospect will be less likely to hold back and will open up and give you a truer picture of his financial situation and his needs.

1.2 Does Good Character Alone Build Trust?

The extent of mis-sold financial products in the UK alone was enough for prospects to develop a barrier of mistrust towards professional advisors. Prospects were sold totally inappropriate products that they did not need. Yet, somehow, those charlatans were able to convince a vast number of clients to buy them.

Those sales people had no:

* Integrity

* Honesty

* Sincerity

* Responsibility for their actions

* Thought for anyone's best interests but their own

Somehow these con-artists appear to have particular skills with which they seem to build trust to make their business. Those same skills can be learned by professionals. Those skills can be used to benefit or defraud. You too can learn how to pass your ideas into your prospects' minds, and save time for both you and your prospect.

It is how you communicate with people that builds instant trust.

1.3 Connect with Your Prospect through Trust

As a result of some bad experiences people have an in-built resistance and scepticism towards others who don't think or act as they do. Our subconscious minds contain internal programs that say:

"I trust people who are similar to me, who think the same way that I think; who see things as I do."

"I don't trust people who are not similar to me, who do not think the same way that I think; who do not see things as I do."

For example, some years ago my friend had been working in Baghdad, Iraq. For his return flight, he decided to transfer from a UK carrier to Iraq Airways simply to fly in an operational Boeing 747 aircraft. During his service in the Royal Air Force he had flown as a passenger in some of the early training flights in the UK. Coincidentally, amongst all the passengers there was just one other Briton. They had never met before but they had an instant trust, an instant bonding. They understood each other completely.

By using an opening statement that the prospect already believes you can overcome his scepticism. If he hears you say something that he believes, his subconscious mind says: "You think the same way as I think." On the other hand, if your first comment is a statement that he disagrees with, the prospect will not trust you.

He might agree with the following opening statements:

* We all want to live a long, healthy life.

* Everyone needs to live somewhere.

* Keeping fit is time-consuming.

* Everyone loves a new car.

Using opening statements similar to these, related to the meeting, your prospect will think: "I understand you."

If you agree with the above statements then you would want your prospect to think the same. You cannot usefully start your presentation until you have built trust in your prospect to the point that he agrees with what you say.

Briefly, here is the difference:

* An amateur will give a presentation to somebody who neither trusts nor believes him.

* A professional will give a presentation to somebody only after that person trusts and believes him.

1.4 Pace

We all think and speak at different speeds. We have different points of view. If you really want to connect with a prospect you need to speak with him at his speed and from his world view and beliefs.

Just think; if you saw your prospect walking in town and you wanted to speak with him you would need to walk alongside him at his pace. If you walked faster than him or slower, you would be unable to communicate properly.

The difference in speeds causes stress and distrust. Not a good formula for bonding with your prospect.

It's the same in your meeting. You need to pace your prospect's thinking, first by telling him something he believes to be true.

1.5 Building Trust Still Further

1.5.1 Smile

Some people smile naturally in such a way that a prospect is immediately set at ease. However, there are those people who haven't smiled for a long time and it shows that they are not relaxed.

But why smile? Sales resistance comes from an in-built human program to survive. It is the survival program that warns us against sudden noises and the possibility of approaching danger. We are all born with this program. Babies know whether someone is safe or dangerous simply because they instinctively look for a smile. When we smile at a baby, they relax and smile back at us. They think they are safe and they set aside their natural resistance to strangers.

The human mind has a program that says, "If someone smiles at me, I can trust them. That person has my best interests at heart." It may seem odd but it does work. A smile will not always create instant trust, belief and rapport, but a frown certainly will not. If you can't smile, save some time and go home. Smiling is the better way, try it yourself.

Think about it another way. A genuine smile is one of our greatest tools for communication and trust. It's simple to do, it's free and it uses different facial muscles, so if you haven't smiled for a long time, you will need to practice.

Try this one: Consciously make an effort to smile at total strangers. Notice how many smile back; you will find a very high percentage of smiling strangers in your life. Now ask yourself: "Is it easier to trust someone who is already smiling with me?"

Practice smiling. It really does work.

1.5.2 Practice with a Smile

Remember, your goal is to get your prospect's mind to believe your message and the information you give. Once he has accepted what you have said and understood the information he can then decide whether or not your message and information will serve his needs.

The process is quite simple:

1. Greet your prospect with a smile. This helps to relax him and it's very effective.

2. Tell your prospect one fact that he can believe.

3. Tell your prospect another fact he can believe.

Try this with a smile:

* "We all want to save for retirement, but we also want to enjoy life now. – smile.

* "Staying at home to look after our children is good, but we all need to make a living." – smile.

* "Buying our first home is exciting, but also it can be scary." – smile.

Building trust only takes seconds. Why? Because people make quick decisions to trust you or not. They don't have time to spend on this part of their life as their brain has so many other things to do.

Hours of conversation and building relationships don't work today; people have little time to talk. They value their time, so now our prospects make instant decisions to preserve their time. The 20th century is over and the methods used in the 1960s no longer apply in today's selling environment. Trust is built almost immediately in our prospect's subconscious mind. That means we have little time to get the message across.

Professionals know that prospects make their decision to believe and trust within seconds. We have to manage that time wisely by using effective trust-building techniques.

1.6 Powerful Words and Phrases to Build Trust

Certain words trigger deep-seated programs that have developed in our subconscious minds as a result of experience and the environment we have lived in. These programs help us to make instant decisions that happen even before the presentation begins.

Let's use the political example. Let's say there are two economists. If you lean towards one economist, you nod your head in agreement when he speaks. There is trust. The economist and you have the same world view on finances. You have already decided to believe what that person says even before he opens his mouth.

However, when an economist from another viewpoint speaks, the moment he moves his lips, you are already sceptical. That person doesn't see the world as you do. There is no trust, no agreement, and no belief. It's just that quick. For instance, if you just think of one economic policy, you immediately have a feeling inside of your mind. Your internal programs lead you to have that feeling.

Now this isn't the only program you have in your mind. You have millions of automatic programs. That's how we are able to function. We don't have to think through everything we do.

We have automatic programs that do this for us; consider the following examples:

* When you drive a car, your sequence of movements, decisions and reactions are almost automatic. And if you change jobs, you will automatically drive back to your old job if you are not paying attention.

* You walk along a street and someone smiles at you, your response is automatic and you return the smile.

* You are browsing in a shop, and a sales assistant comes to you and says: "Can I help you?"... Your automatic response is to reply with: "Oh no. I am just looking."

* You walk into an elevator and there is a stranger already there, you automatically stand as far away as possible, but still face the stranger so as not to appear rude.

* Someone asks you, "How are you?" Without even thinking, your automatic reply is: "Oh, just surviving" or "Very well, thank you." Irrespective of any challenges you may be going through, your response depends on your internal programs.

It makes sense that certain words and phrases activate these automatic programs within our prospects' minds.

When used in an appropriate way, these words and phrases can make it easier to build instant trust and present our message and information.

Here are some word phrases taken from Tom "Big Al" Schreiter's book, *How To Get Instant Trust, Belief, Influence And Rapport! 13 Ways To Create Open Minds By Talking To The Subconscious Mind*. These simple word phrases and programs make it easy for prospects to stay in rapport with you throughout your presentations.

Survival

Some of the important programs in our mind are for survival. Many decisions we make are based upon survival. Here are some examples:

* Prospects' scepticism derives from their survival program.

* Prospects don't like being deceived into losing money or time.

* Scepticism is a defensive barrier that a prospect can use to protect himself.

A sceptical prospect that doesn't trust or believe you will not give you his serious attention or agree with what you say. By using certain powerful words you can use the prospect's survival program to get him to accept your message and information in total trust.

* Most people would like to know these powerful words.

* If they knew them most people would use these powerful words over and over again.

* These powerful words help most people to become super-communicators.

* If you are like most people, you are keen to learn these powerful words.

Here they are:

"Most people."

As in nature, one of our ways of surviving is to stay with the group. We know that to survive we don't want to think of ourselves as being alone outside the group. There is safety in numbers and when a prospect hears you say "most people," he thinks to himself: "Am I part of most people, or am I part of a few people? I need to be part of most people because it is much safer. I don't want to risk being alone."

As humans we decide to do what most people do. Do you think it works? Well, see if this sounds like "Most people" to you. A famous toothpaste manufacturer simply says: "4 out of 5 dentists recommend ..." And instantly we think that toothpaste is pretty good. Quick, wasn't it? And this was all before the facts and presentation. We make decisions every day based upon "most people." For example, what do you think when you see two restaurants side by side? One restaurant is busy, the other is empty.

Yes, that decision was pretty quick, wasn't it? Therefore, we need to put some examples of "most people" in our opening statements to prospects.

For example, doesn't it sound nicer to start with:

"Most families want to be secure."

"Most investors want to protect their capital."

"Most people want to limit their insurance premiums."

Your prospect, upon hearing these phrases, feels you understand him and he will then listen further with an open mind.

"Everybody Knows and Everybody Says."

"Most people" are not the only words that get people to agree. "Everybody knows" and "Everybody says" also work well. Our aim is to get people to believe what we say. There are two ways to get people to believe what we say:

1. Browbeat them into submission with endless facts, PowerPoint presentations, research reports, graphs, proof, testimonials and other mind-numbing drivel. In the end, our prospects will probably say: "I give up. OK, I'll believe you."

2. Simply command your prospect's subconscious mind to instantly believe what you will say next with just these two sets of words: "Everybody knows" and "Everybody says." No further discussion or proof is necessary.

Method 2 sounds a lot easier on you and your prospect. So let's use powerful word phrases simply to command our prospect to accept whatever we say as true with no further proof necessary.

Most people reading this will want to know these types of phrases. And everybody knows that if we knew these phrases, we would want to use them over and over again. And, everybody says that we need to learn these phrases quickly so we can earn more money. It's pretty obvious, isn't it? "Everybody knows" and "Everybody says" lead people instantly to accept what we say as true. Here is what is happening in your listener's mind. When you say these powerful phrases, the subconscious mind runs the following program or script:

"Everybody knows ... am I part of everybody ... or am I part of nobody? Nobody is part of nobody, so I must be part of everybody. And if everybody knows it, then that would mean that I know it, and if I know it, well, then it must be true!"

This is how our mind works; it's embarrassing but true. As long as what we say is reasonable, the prospect will instantly accept what we say as true, no further proof is required.

The same works for "Everybody says." Here is the script our minds execute when someone says, "Everybody says." "Everybody says ... hmmm, am I part of everybody ... or am I part of nobody? Nobody is part of nobody, so I must be part of everybody. And if everybody says it, then that would mean that I say it, and if I say it, well, then it must be true, because I am not a liar!" In just that moment, we decide that what is said must be true.

Here are some examples:

* Everybody says they don't have time to research and become an expert on all the investment options.

* Everybody knows that investing can be risky.

"Everybody knows" and "Everybody says" are two power phrases that you can use to quickly get your prospect to believe your message. This is important, because these phrases tend to bypass your prospect's internal defence programs such as:

* Scepticism of strangers.

* Negative past sales experiences.

* It's too good to be true.

* There's got to be a catch here somewhere.

Now it is easy for you to communicate and get your prospects to believe what you have to say.

"Well, You Know How …"

This is another powerful phrase that helps us get our prospects to believe us. Simply put "Well, you know how" before you present your facts and most prospects will automatically run this little script in their subconscious minds: "Well, you know how ... If he says I already know how, then it must be true, because what I know is true."

That may sound odd, but it's how we think. It is amazing, and true, when we say "Well, you know how," our prospect starts immediately nodding and agreeing with us, even before we tell our prospect what we are going to say next!

And it gets better. Most people tend to start smiling as you say these words. So consider this. Instead of talking to a sceptical prospect, why not say "Well, you know how" first, and then watch your prospect lean forward, smile, and start nodding "Yes" in total agreement with what you are going to say next.

Most people reading this would like to see some examples, because everybody knows that the best way to learn is from examples and everybody says that just a few examples could help us think creatively. If you didn't catch it, re-read the previous paragraph. That was easy enough, wasn't it?

* Well, you know how we don't want to risk big losses in our investments?

* Well, you know how we want a diversified portfolio to spread the risks?

"Well, you know how" makes it easy to get our ideas into our prospects' minds. And it's quick.

Well, you know how we don't want to waste our time talking to prospects who don't believe us? Now, that was easy, wasn't it?

"There is an old saying ..."

Yes, there are a lot of old sayings. For example:

* There is an old saying that you should never believe what people say, but only believe what people do.

* There is an old saying that you should never trust a political promise.

* There is an old saying that bad news sells.

* There is an old saying that you want your investments to work for you instead of you working for your investments.

* There is an old saying that amateur investors get professional advice AFTER they invest.

What's going on here? Well, when we say the words: "There is an old saying" ... inside our prospect's subconscious mind the following script is activated: "If anybody, anywhere, at any time says, 'There is an old saying,' ... then it must be true because it is an old saying!"

That's how our subconscious mind makes quick decisions. Our minds have better things to do than to question and think about every statement. So our mind sets up some shortcuts to make thinking about everything a lot easier. One of the shortcuts is if anyone says "There is an old saying," ... then the mind automatically accepts it as true, so the mind can get on to other more important things. Well, you know how examples would make this easier?

Let The Mystery Begin!

So let's put a couple of these powerful words together and see exactly how we can get prospects to open up their minds to hear the good things we say. The more powerful words phrases we use, the easier it will be for our prospect. Most people would like to see some examples now:

 * "Well, you know how we hate paying too much for a new car?"

 * "Most people want a good deal that saves them money."

 * "Everybody knows it is fun to brag to your friends about what a great price you got on your new car."

How does the prospect feel now? This is good bonding with the car advisor.

Or maybe the car advisor could have said this:

 * "There is an old saying that high volume dealerships have the lowest prices."

 * "Everybody knows that selling hundreds of cars a month will lower the price per car."

 * "Most people would love to take advantage of these savings." (Smile)

Turn Off The "Advisor Alarm" With This Phrase.

People are programmed to be wary of professionals who have an agenda and want to sell you something. Nobody likes to be sold, but people love to buy. By putting the control of the information flow in their hands, you get the prospect to feel as if they are buying instead of feeling that they are being sold.

When someone is giving a presentation, they are 'selling' to you. When you ask questions, and they answer your questions, you are buying. See the difference? What question can you ask that will change their perception of you? Try this:

"What would you like to know first?" Instead of pitching and presenting, you put them in the question-asking mode. It's easy and it is polite.

Nobody enjoys a one-way conversation where the professional is talking at us so, as soon as possible, ask the question:

"What would you like to know first?"

Do you know what is really fun?

Your prospect will actually tell you what he wants to know first, and you will be talking about things that really matter to him.

Give A Sincere Compliment.

This is not quite as simple as it seems. An obvious compliment makes the prospect feel a greater sense of insecurity.

So don't make obvious compliments such as:

* You are looking good today.

* My, what a nice house.

* I like the way you dress.

* You're a very intelligent person.

These compliments create an even bigger barrier of scepticism in your prospect. Most people are embarrassed to accept an obvious compliment.

A less obvious compliment shows that you care enough to look deeper, and see something most people wouldn't notice.

Let's look at the above compliments and try some less obvious versions:

* You are always smiling. Where do you find the energy to smile while raising four children and looking after a husband?

* These wood floors look good. Were they difficult to install?

* I like that silk scarf. Where did you buy it?

23

* I see you read *Business Weekly*. How long have you subscribed?

* Your investments are well-documented and organized. Were you always good at finances?

Did you notice how we included a question with each less obvious compliment? When you ask a question after your compliment, it takes the pressure off the prospect. They don't have to thank you for the compliment. Instead, they have a question to answer, and that's a lot more comfortable for the prospect.

Encourage Your Prospect To Talk About Himself Immediately!

Dale Carnegie pointed this out brilliantly in his book, *How to Win Friends and Influence People*. Given a chance to talk about himself, with a willing listener (you), your prospect cannot resist such an opportunity. For most people, these golden moments are few and far between. Once your prospect has an opportunity to talk about his ideas, dreams, goals, and problems, he will feel more comfortable with you. You simply lead your prospect into talking about himself by just asking an open question that doesn't lead to a 'yes' or 'no' answer!

Your prospect will take it from there. If you can't think of a question, here are a few to start with:

* Have you lived here long?

* Where did you see my ad?

* What part of my ad was interesting to you?

* How long have you known John?

* How long have you had this problem?

* Do you like to travel?

* How early do you have to leave in the morning to beat the traffic?

* What would you do with a lot more free time?

* How do you feel about investing?

* How does your spouse feel about investing?

It's simple, isn't it? The bottom line is this: If our prospects are scared, resistant and suspicious of us, then our presentation will fall on sceptical ears and that's bad. But if our prospects are talking about themselves, everything in their world is just fine. They are happy, they feel in control. After all, how could they be sceptical when fascinating people, such as themselves, are talking? The more you let your prospect talk, the easier it is for him to trust you and for him to think of you as an interesting person. If you do all the talking he could think of you as a boring person.

A Simple Question That Might Dispel Trust.

When you ask "Why?" you demonstrate your interest, and your prospect talks more to answer you. However, you have to be very careful when you ask the "Why?" question.

Remember when you were young and you did something wrong? Your parents or teacher would ask you: "WHY did you do that?" Not only did you feel bad, but you also had to explain truthfully WHY you did it. This question put you on the defensive and, well, you know how no trust was created with that question?

Now, let's imagine you are talking to a prospect and you are presenting on a particular product. Your prospect has just stated that his previous purchase was another product.

You ask:

"So why did you buy that product last time?" And now your prospect is telling you all the good reasons he bought that particular product, convincing himself that it was a good decision. It will be difficult for you to create trust later in the conversation when you tell your prospect that your products are a better choice.

So use "Why" very carefully.

It's not helpful when your prospect has to explain his reason for not buying what you have to offer.

"Is It Hard For People To Believe You?"

Most people know the answer is: "No."

Everybody knows that it is easy to get people to believe the good things you say. In this chapter we have covered the starter techniques that lead to a better conversation, better presentation and better belief; all summed up as ... trust!

1. Tell your prospect facts that you both can agree upon.

2. Pace your speed to match your prospect.

3. Tell your prospect two facts you both can agree upon.

4. Smile.

5. Most people.

6. Everybody knows.

7. Everybody says.

8. Well, you know how.

9. There is an old saying.

10. What would you like to know first?

11. Sincere compliment.

12. Encourage your prospect to do the talking.

13. Avoid a "WHY" question that your prospect has to defend.

Trust is built very quickly. In just seconds, the automatic programs in our minds decide whether or not to trust and believe a person. All this happens with the automatic programs in our minds.

There is an old saying: "Dogs know who to bite." Some people describe trust as a feeling, a vibe, a connection, but now we know that the decision to trust is not some random event; it is something we can control.

Are you feeling powerful? Are you ready to change people's lives with your ideas instead of your ideas bouncing off their foreheads?

With 13 ways to create the trust you've always wanted, the rest is up to you.

Points to ponder

1. Clients buy you first, then a service or product.

2. If you win a client on price you will lose a client on price; people buy from people they trust.

3. Price is only an issue if there is a lack of perceived value or service.

"Animals can learn,
but people can learn to discern."

~ Mark Twain ~

2. Understand Your Client's Secret Language

2.1 Learning the Secret Languages

Do you sometimes find that your message is not getting across to your client?

You need to be aware that what you say can mean different things depending on the prospect's 'secret language,' how he or she understands the world and communicates to others.

Think of a group of people, such as your family or friends; you know that they are all unique. As we saw in chapter 1, people think, speak and behave differently. They dress differently and they respond or react to different experiences in different ways. It is our temperament, or personality, that defines who we are. Naturally, how we behave is a combination of nature, the personality we are born with, and nurture, the environment in which we have been programmed to think and act. Even identical twins can behave differently as they grow up.

To understand your prospect's 'secret language,' you have to accept that they are not like you. When we understand ourselves and others we are able to overcome difficulties in communication. When you have a problem in communicating with a client you will find it difficult to work with him, especially if you do not understand what is going on inside the client's mind. Top professionals know themselves and know how to deal with the different languages that people present through their behaviour.

It is possible to give a presentation to one client, and receive a certain response. You can give exactly the same presentation to somebody else and have a totally different response. They each heard what you said through the 'filter' of their personality and experience. It is not that one or the other misunderstood you; they just understood differently what you said.

You can understand people and their 'secret language' when you are fully aware of human behaviour and what motivates them. There is a simple way to recognise a person's 'secret language.' This will lead you to appreciate how people are motivated. You will also see how relationships work and how they can be made more effective by reducing misunderstanding and conflict.

Human behaviour has been studied by philosophers and scientists for many centuries. Some studies have focused on abnormal behaviour - what is wrong with a person - to identify personality "disorders." However, during the last 100 years other behaviour models have been developed based on normal human behaviour. Some of these models are objective and descriptive rather than subjective and judgmental as they used to be.

We are all unique. We have different characteristics that describe our personality. Some of us flourish under pressure while others wither and fade. Some like to stand out and be noticed whereas some prefer to take refuge in a crowd. Some people look for confrontation while others prefer peace and harmony. One is not right or wrong, it's just how we are made – our personality. All personalities have good and bad points.

This is where it is important for professionals to recognise the different behaviour patterns and responses in their clients. You will notice if a person is outgoing or reserved. Similarly you can see the difference between one person who wants to get on with the business at hand and another who is keen to talk about people or relationships.

Your success as a professional comes down to how you relate to people. If you don't know your clients or understand how they think, how can you expect to help them in making important decisions?

Some models of human behaviour use colours to describe the dominant characteristics, the strengths of the personality. In one model, the primary colours red, blue and yellow are used to describe three dominant personality traits and green describes the fourth. Our personalities comprise a mixture of all four colours, but for each of us one colour is usually dominant over the others.

RED personalities are outgoing and task-oriented. They like to be the boss; they are managers, organisers, politicians. They are focused on getting things done. They like competition and winning. They love recognition; they are not good listeners because they know the answers. In financial matters they look for the "bottom line" – what's the profit, what do I get out of this? As you develop a relationship with this type of personality remember to focus on results. Respect them even though they are not the best at respecting other people.

The language you use with the red personality is something like: These are the choices, you make the decision; you can be in charge; this is what it's worth.

BLUE personalities are outgoing and people-oriented. They love meeting people, parties, fun, and adventure. The last stranger they met is their best friend. They do not listen because they are so talkative. Blues treat laws as suggestions. They do not follow up because they are too busy meeting new people. They are the big-picture people with lots of activity. They are focused on what others think of them; they revel in admiration and recognition.

The language you use with the blue personality is something like: This is an exciting chance for you to talk with people; it's party time; there will be lots of travel.

YELLOW personalities are reserved and people-oriented; they enjoy relationships and love to help and hug others. They see products and services as being there to help people. As leaders, they see themselves as being there to help their team or subordinates. They try to avoid conflict wherever possible. They tend to set aside their own work or interests if they see that someone needs help. As you develop a relationship with this type of personality, remember the importance of friendliness and sincerity towards them.

The language you use with the yellow personality is something like: We need your help; would you like to help these people?

GREEN personalities are reserved and work-oriented. They depend on consistency and quality information for decisions. They are motivated to seek out more information. It is difficult to close with a green personality until they have all the facts. They take time to check all the facts so they have all the right answers. They want to be correct and accurate, and if that takes time, so be it. To develop a relationship with them you need to demonstrate integrity and trustworthiness.

The language you use for the green personality is something like: We need your opinion; would you like to check these facts? You will find more information on our website.

2.2 Dealing with Different Personalities

The stories on the following pages show how I adapt my approach to work successfully with different personality types.

2.2.1 Working with a Tough Decision-maker

Some years ago a friend of mine was involved in marketing. He was trying to set up a sponsorship deal before the cut-off date at the beginning of the football season. He had tried for 18 months without success. On paper, it was a no-brainer because the Premiership football team and the deal 'ticked all the boxes.' He desperately wanted an opportunity to explain the deal to the right person, the one who could make the decision. Yet, somehow, he just couldn't get through to speak with him. The challenge for him was that time was running out.

When he asked me to help, the first thing I did was to phone the decision-maker's PA and I made it my goal to build trust and rapport immediately. I used the words in the previous chapter, as well as using some advanced questioning skills such as, "I am just curious..." followed by an appropriate question. These four magic words unlock the secrets in a person's subconscious mind, and you can find out any information you want. For example:

"Is your boss impatient or does he have plenty of time?"

"Does he make quick decisions?"

"Is he quite friendly or more work-focused?"

From her answers to these questions, it was obvious to me that her boss was a driven, work-focused person; a dominant red personality type. She connected me through to him and, in a 20-second phone call, he agreed to an appointment for the next day. In that phone call I used the 4, 4, 5 exact-word process outlined in this book.

I met him the next day and asked him WHAT he wanted from the deal. There was no small talk, no talk about family, etc. We got straight to the point. He told me what he wanted, I knew we could deliver, and bingo! A seven-minute meeting resulted in a win for everyone. At the end of the meeting, the decision-maker said to me: "Young man, this is how all business should be done; fast, efficient and clean. One of the easiest sales I have ever done." He went on to say: "Tell your colleague that the reason I have avoided him for 18 months is that I am not interested in going to lunch with him, going on a five-day trip to Vegas, or playing golf in Spain. I just wanted to make sure I could get the business done quickly."

The point of this story is that my friend is an outgoing person with a highly interactive blue type of personality. He sees doing business the way he likes to do business, like many sales people do, without first considering the needs of the client and their personality.

2.2.2 Meeting an Extrovert Leader

A few years ago, I was approached by the leader of a women's cricket team. She wanted some help with a presentation she was to give to schools. After spending some time on the phone, it was clear to me that she had an interactive, blue type of personality and she was very much people–focused; she was very sociable. We arranged to meet for lunch and I showed her techniques on how to deliver her presentation.

Later she told me that her presentation went brilliantly and was well-accepted at the schools where she spoke. We had a further meeting, again over lunch, where I listened to her concerns about the communication issues within the women's team, and later that week I was offered a contract to work with the cricket team. We covered communication between the coach and captain, the captain and players, and the players and the media.

The cricket team has since become very successful in Great Britain and Ireland. Earlier they had been ranked as one of the lesser teams, but with the additional skills they had learned and with the same players, they became a world-class team. I take no credit for their performance on the field, how they bowled or batted, but I was able to help them in the aspects of communication and features such as how the mind makes decisions, or how to perform under pressure and how to get the best out of people through communication. My relationship with the team began because I understood the personality of the leader and her 'secret language.'

2.2.3 Helping a Sensitive Senior Law Partner

I was travelling to Lords to see England play in the test match against India. I was sitting in the first class carriage drinking coffee. By chance, opposite me was another member of the MCC (Marylebone Cricket Club). After acknowledging one another it became clear to me that his soft, gentle and slightly slower-paced conversation indicated he had an empathetic, yellow type of personality.

As the conversation came to what we did for a living, he explained the challenges he had with his law firm and how some of the fee-earners were struggling to get new business. Also, he said that with the introduction of Tesco Law in 2009 (the phrase 'Tesco Law' was coined to describe the idea that buying legal services would be as easy as supermarket shopping), it meant that anyone could buy a law firm. At the time of writing this book, the Co-op was the largest supplier of law firms in the UK, with many small firms either merging or going out of business.

My question to him was: "Would you like to help your staff?" He really did want to help his staff and this was the key to his asking me to help him and his firm.

I pursued the questioning with:

* "Is it important to you to help your staff?"

* "Do you want to help them reduce their stress when looking for new business?"

* "Do you want to help them to get more clients so they can be more profitable?"

Sensitive people genuinely want to help, they are good listeners and they are brilliant at completing a task.

2.2.4 Facts for a Conscientious Financial Team Leader

I met Sean, a Chartered Financial Advisor running a region with over 250 financial advisors. I was introduced to him by one of his advisors, after we had been out to lunch. The meeting with Sean was in his office; it was pristine. He was dressed immaculately, his Mont Blanc fountain pen indicated an eye for quality; a green personality type. From the thoroughness of his questions, it was obvious to me that he was very conscientious and had strong organisational skills. I respected his probing questions and his attention to detail. He trusted me enough to ask me to speak to his region's advisors at the Belfry Golf and Country Club in the Midlands. To win Sean's confidence, he needed to hear from me the words:

"I will go through a comprehensive structured program to give your advisors a systematic approach to get more clients, with the exact words and phrases to use in the following scenarios:

* To get automatic referrals,

* The exact words to fill your diary when using the telephone,

* And quick and easy closing skills."

Whenever the owner/director/manager of an organisation wants me to coach their people or speak, I frequently ask them for a testimonial.

Six months after incredible results for his advisors, Sean gave me a video testimonial which has since opened doors for me to work with many other financial services companies. He has helped me to develop a programme to help financial advisors at all levels to get better results. The key to getting his confidence and instruction was that I answered his questions with quality responses. I over-delivered on all the training and I developed training programs with a step-by-step process to present them.

Points to ponder

1. People do not do things to deliberately upset you, but they do things within their nature.

2. Opposites attract then opposites attack; look for the good in each personality.

3. Task-focused people make decisions on evidence; people-focused people make decisions on feelings.

"Coming together is a beginning;
keeping together is progress;
working together is success."

~ Henry Ford ~

3. Networking and Prospecting

3.1 Networking Meetings

Networking meetings can provide an excellent forum at which professionals can speak with authority, and can also come to be known as problem-solvers when it comes to advice in their own profession. I have mentored people in particular clubs in the past and this has given me a good understanding of what works and what doesn't work at these networking meetings.

In this chapter, I'm not prescribing exactly what you should promote or discuss at a meeting; I have made a CD in which about 20 people, in a live workshop, give examples that they use; these could be relevant. However, I do cover comprehensively what to do before, during and after the meeting. In my experience I have found that more business is generated by booking a one-to-one meeting with people I meet at these gatherings. Also, with ad-hoc meetings you could always ask for the delegate list. If a list is available, you could target your research to the relevant people that fit your business. Otherwise, without preparation, it could end up simply as a market at which everyone tries to sell to each other.

When you attend events where you don't know many people, here are a few tips for you to consider:

* Where refreshments are served and you carry a drink, hold it in your left hand so you are ready to shake hands with prospects. Remember it is all about the prospect and building rapport.

* Design your own professional name badge and keep it on your left side. In this way you are not dependent on a sticky paper one that the organisers may hand you. Remember, irrespective of the function, you are a professional representing yourself and your company.

* It is important for you to be very selective of the networking meetings you attend. For instance, it is quite possible that several delegates at a particular event could be from the same or similar profession; this could be at least embarrassing and uncomfortable for all.

* Some start-up networking meetings might not include people with an appropriate income profile relevant to your business. However, don't make quick assumptions, because we all know you could meet people who are well-connected to valuable referrals that do match your business.

At some breakfast meetings, a 60-second weekly presentation is required.

So let's talk about your 60-second presentation that will help you to stimulate interest and a response from the audience. You are not there to sell your service but merely to get people to say "How?" or "Tell me more." As we know, people make decisions immediately; the first few seconds mean everything. There is a simple rule that respected advertising companies use, as well as TV and radio broadcasters. This is how it works:

1. Fact

2. Fact

3. Hook

For example, when I am promoting presentation skills, I use this:

Speaking in public can be stressful (fact number 1), and it could give you sleepless nights (fact number 2); however, some people have figured out how to deliver a perfect stress-free presentation every time (hook).

Anyone who has ever struggled with a presentation will agree with the first 2 statements, and there is an open-loop technique which requires the hearer's mind to think "Who" and "How." The facts need to be non-controversial, short and void of jargon or technical terminology; otherwise, the listener will switch off.

The hook needs to be a third-party recommendation, avoiding these words: I, Me or My. As soon as you use these words in your speech, it raises the salesman alarm. Once you have that opening - which takes a few seconds - you need a short story, which gives credence to your statement.

This is how we tell a story. I will use the name Jack, as an example. There are 5 points to a short story:

1. People meet Jack.

2. People like Jack.

3. Jack has a problem.

4. Jack overcomes the problem.

5. Jack becomes a hero.

So your story could be along the lines of:

"I received a postcard from some clients of mine this week from the Bahamas. They are a lovely couple, John and Sally. John found out he had cancer a year ago, and because he had critical illness insurance cover, he was paid out £150,000 which allowed him to pay off his mortgage. He has recently been given the all-clear from the cancer and, as a result, has taken a holiday."

This could be a short story, where you promote a product instead of selling it.

To follow on from the story, you introduce one sentence about your own business in third party terms. Starting:

"At ABC Financial Services, we listen to our clients' needs, as we realise everyone is an individual and we do not charge for a meeting."

The close could be: A simple contrast close of giving the audience the choice of life as it is (not pleasant) or business with me. Here goes....

"So what is easier for you, to continue without having the adequate cover, worrying at night, or to have a coffee with an advisor at no cost, to give you total peace of mind?"

3.2 7 Networking 'Gems'

We all know the importance of networking and you may already be part of a networking organisation, breakfast session group or regular business collaboration. Yet the most surprising thing of all is the lack of networking skills employed at such functions; and worse still, the poor level of follow-up after the event.

In speaking with networkers over the years and coaching many of them, I've often been staggered to learn that people tend to see the result of a good networking session as the accumulation of business cards, and that the follow-up consists of getting the cards transferred to a database or card filing system. What a waste of time, energy and future opportunity!

Here then, of the scores of tools available, are the top 7 networking tools that professionals should be acutely aware of and use frequently.

3.3 Top 7 Networking Tools

1 – The Website Question

This is a great tool that's so easy to execute and works one hundred percent of the time. When you meet someone at your next event, ask about the person's website. Listen carefully to their description and comments, then inquire about the details - this will always result in the exchange of business cards. Then pop the real 'website question.' Ask them if they'd like some feedback on their site in exchange for some feedback on your own. Be careful with this one if you are in the business of creating websites; the request could be taken as a sales pitch and therefore you must make it clear that it's purely for two-way feedback, but for any other business or occupation, it's gold dust. The reason is:

* The feedback gives you a reason to contact the person.

* It ensures that they actually look at your site carefully.

* It creates an opportunity to ask relevant questions about people they know.

2 – The Most Powerful Question

You will be aware of the difference between open and closed questions. An open question starts up dialogue and normally begins with what, how, when, where, why and who; whereas a closed question is 'black and white' requesting only a yes or no response. Initial questions such as 'Are you..?' and 'Will you..?' and so on.

However, do you know that the most powerful question is very simply: 'Why…?'

It's the one question that is rarely asked as the opening of a dialogue. For instance, if you buy a new car, usually a salesperson's opening question is a 'What…?' question such as 'What's your budget…?' 'What model…?' 'What colour…?' Yet what if they were to open the dialogue with a 'Why..?' question: 'Why did you choose us?' or 'Why have you decided to change your car?' The answers would be far more revealing and offer you far greater leverage in the sales dialogue.

It's just the same with networking. Ask: 'Why did you come here today?' and 'Why have you decided to do more networking?' The answers will provide you with much better insights for discussion and the development of mutual trust than the more common, rather superficial topics raised in a networking interaction.

3 - Proactive Listening

We tend to be acutely aware of the need for this tool in a dialogue, yet so often we are not very good at implementing it. In proactive listening, there are three things you can do which are simple and highly effective.

But why is making the effort to listen carefully so important?

There is nothing more boring than having to listen to someone you are not that interested in, yet this in itself is a problem. The more bored you become, the more your expression shows in your eyes and your overall body language gives the game away. The result is a waste of another networking opportunity on both sides. When others are interested in us, we tend to subconsciously want to reciprocate provided we are fed with good questions (re-

read previous tool.) To listen well is simply good manners and part of building trust; it includes:

* Nod with sincere eye contact.

* Listen in such a way that you would be able to repeat it to someone else.

* Avoid the temptation to look elsewhere, at other people, even for a fleeting moment.

Of course you will meet people who have no idea of good listening skills and may start to bore you, but politely raising your hand to indicate you have a question will normally make the other person pause to allow you to ask your great question.

There's no question about it that the more we are prepared to proactively listen, the more the other person likes us and trusts us. As you use the other tools listed here, you will be on a 'winning wicket.'

4 - The Most Well-Received Question

It is curious how we as humans find it difficult to ask for what we want. It may be lack of confidence, fear of upsetting the other person or simply we are unaware of what the best question is.

The best question I refer to is: 'How could I be of most help to you and your business?' Think about this. If you were at a networking event and someone asked you that question, would it delight you or disappoint you? It's hardly likely to be the latter.

Of course this is music to your ears. So with this in mind shouldn't you ask the question quite early on in the dialogue? Once the other party has told you gleefully what help they ideally want - and you have courteously made some notes - maybe on the back of their business card, don't you think it more than likely that they would want to reciprocate and ask you a similar question?

5 - Lowering the Defence Screen

Networking sometimes calls for the creation of a 'defence screen.' This would occur when you feel you are being 'sold to' by the other person, or when you speak with someone who has their screen in use. Situations like this can be a challenge. This is where you use the 'Third Party Approach' tool.

It goes like this. You and the other person have met and you've exchanged business cards. Then they ask you what you do or what your business does. Naturally you would want to reply with a 'Why...' question first, such as 'Why you do what you do.' But rather than refer it all to the listener, you go around the person by referring to a third party which will lower your defence screen.

So you may say. 'If you know any other businesses who would be interested in what I offer, this is how I can help them...'

By talking around the person and referring to a third party, the person you are networking with doesn't feel threatened or put on the spot. It makes it easier for them to ask you more questions and even think that they themselves would actually be quite interested in some help.

6 - The Classic Tease

There's a well-known 1970s detective called Columbo played by Peter Falk who appeared to be not very bright, yet he was extremely intelligent and a master of human psychology. One of his techniques was to tease the suspect with a really key question then suddenly change the subject completely - usually to observe the suspect's reaction to the important question while he innocuously chatted about something quite superficial.

This approach works well in a slightly different way in networking circles.

Make a comment about something you do that sounds exciting, extraordinary, daring, different or simply amazing, then change the subject. You will know you've hit the bull's-eye when the other party brings you back to what you previously said and asks questions about it. This also allows you to ostensibly respond to their interest rather than your interest.

Imagine you run an office services business and you say something like, '...and of course, all we have to do for happy clients is implement 3 simple techniques that impact their turnover by at least thirty percent...' (Smile, pause.) Then, 'Tell me; is this your first visit to this group?'

At least half the people you do this with will ask about the 3 simple techniques. If you are dealing with someone who seems to ignore the tease, after a few minutes repeat it in another way. Usually this will produce the all-important tease-response question. If it hasn't, politely move on to speak with someone else!

7 - Finding a Reason to Stay Connected

This tool is all about finding a reason to call the person who has just given you their business card after the event. Making a habit of calling everyone who gives you a card is absolutely vital if you are a seasoned and entrepreneurial networker. However, if you don't have a reason when you call them, it can feel a bit embarrassing.

So, make sure you have a reason! The way you do this is to use most of the above tools and listen out for something that they say where a good question pops into your mind, but at the same time you delay asking the question until you follow up. What's also critical is that you write down the question, usually on the back of their card - or on the front of it, if there's no space on the back.

By the way, a final point about exchanging cards. When someone hands you their card, do take a few seconds to actually read it in front of them. Also flip it over to see if there's anything on the back. I find it so rude when I offer my card to someone and they ignore it completely and slip it in their back pocket, probably with all the other cards they received that day. They may as well have put it in the bin - at least that's what I would have felt at the time!!

We in the West can learn something about the procedure used in the Far East regarding the exchange of business cards. They present their card with two hands. The receiver reads both sides of the card in front of the giver before doing the same with their card for an equal level of interest and response. This is all about respect for the other person.

Points to ponder

1. Be interested, not interesting.
2. Find a reason to connect and stay connected.
3. Let people know what you can do for them, not what you do.

"Nothing in the world can take the place of persistence"

~ President Calvin Coolidge ~

4. Telephone Calls

Over the years, the skill of making appointments on the phone has diminished. Many people have hidden behind emails, direct mail and other internet-based advertising. It seems that people have become afraid of using the phone. At seminars, I often speak about the 6 levels of communication. Here they are, in reverse order, for creating rapport and giving you a chance to get more business:

6th – Email/Text

5th – Letter

4th – Telephone Call

3rd – Skype/FaceTime

2nd – Face-to-Face Meeting

1st – Meeting with Food

As we know, meeting face-to-face or over food is the highest level of rapport. From experience, people will only have a meal with people they feel comfortable about. However, the best way to arrange a level 1 or 2 meeting is via a level 4 phone call.

So why do people fear the phone?

Many people fear the phone when really it is the fear of rejection that causes the discomfort. So would it be OK if I give you, word-for-word, what to say and how to use the phone rejection-free? Let's start from the beginning. The only way we know if we are successful at making phone calls is by monitoring and keeping good records. If we don't keep records, we can't break records, and we need to maintain the ratios so we can predict our income and improve our performance.

Key Point - Use the Law of Averages

Your success in selling and how well your telephone session goes are governed by the Law of Averages or the Law of Ratios.

Research shows that when the average amount of initial advice fee is between £500 and £2000 (let's say an average of £1,000), and if you get 5 people to say "Yes" and agree to see you, certain scenarios will result. So let's use this as an example; keep in mind that this is a general approximation, and when you measure your results, this could be different.

1. One client will not be there.

Think how de-motivating it is if you turn up for your appointment and your client is out or unable to see you. Turn this into a positive - understand the law of averages and **plan for 20% of your clients not to be there to see you.** Of course, these are very low figures compared with many professionals.

2. One client will not listen to your story.

Of the remaining four clients, you won't be able to tell your story or give your presentation to at least one client because:

* The client doesn't like you or trust you.

* You don't like the client.

* You realise they are not a good client.

* Some other reason you did not anticipate.

3. Of the remaining three, one client will buy.

Your own personal ratio may be higher or lower depending upon your skill level, but whatever your ratio, it will remain constant unless you improve.

Think about it, how many clients do you need to speak to on the phone to get those 5 "Yes" answers? Based on this Law of Averages, it is possible to work out the exact cost (£) of each call you make.

For example:

As we said earlier, the average amount of initial advice fee from one sale is between £500 and £2,000; let's say £1,000.

You have to make 10 calls to secure 5 appointments. As above, of the 5 appointments made, one client will not be there, one will not listen. Of the 3 people that see you, one will buy. Therefore 10 calls secured you 1 sale, your average profit generated from one sale is £1,000, averaging out to £100 per call.

21-Day Plan

You will find a template Telephone Success Call Sheet later in this chapter. Begin to use it and stick with it for 21 days. This will show your average ratio with which to work. Remember, your own personal ratio may be higher or lower than others. Your goal is to improve and become even more professional.

By continually using your Telephone Success Call Sheet, you will be able to judge your performance; if your ratio shows a decline, it may be time for you to re-examine your script.

LOOK AFTER YOUR ACTIVITY AND THE PRODUCTION WILL LOOK AFTER ITSELF.

To recap:

* Sell the 'appointment,' not the product or service.

* Sell the "Yes."

* 10 calls = 5 meetings arranged.

* 5 clients = 1 won't be there, 1 won't want to listen; out of the remaining 3, 1 will buy.

* Don't call it an 'appointment'. Appointment = pain and money. Use 'drop-by' or 'meet.'

PRACTICE THIS TECHNIQUE FOR 21 DAYS.

7 Rules before making a call:

1. Have a clean desk.

2. Don't accept incoming calls or talk to anyone.

3. Make the decision not to leave the desk.

4. Once you have picked up your phone, don't put it down. (Landline)

5. Time between phone calls – no more than 60 seconds.

6. Sit down or stand up in front of a mirror for posture. Smile while you speak.

7. Make a "Do not disturb" sign, and put it in full sight.

7 Rules during a call:

1. Match your speaking speed to that of the person you are calling.

2. Match your tone of voice to that of the person you are calling. (Soft, loud, coarse, gentle)

3. Never plan to talk for more than 1 hour.

4. Depending on the client, never ask if they have time to speak. (They could say "No.")

5. Don't confirm appointments, as this could make it easy for your prospect to say "I'm glad you called, can we reschedule this appointment?"

6. Keep statistics.

7. Stick to your script so you know what works; you can only manage what you can measure.

4 Stages of a Call:

1. Opening

2. Rapport

3. Ice breaker

4. Appointment

Telephone Script

The most successful script I have used with professionals over the last 20 years is definitely 7-9-4-4-5, and that can easily be shortened to 4-4-5. You probably wonder what these numbers mean. Well, these are the exact words for you to use and how to deliver them, so it is clinically clear what to say.

So let's start with the 7 words once you have completed the opening, which is introducing each other: **"Is this a good time for you?"** I suggest you always use this with clients that you know well. If the answer is: "No," a simple response: *"When would be a good time to speak? It is important."* At this stage, the inquisitive mind will say: "Well, what is it?" and you will have a chance to speak.

The next 9 words are: **"(Their first name), you are probably wondering why I am calling."** And their response will always be: "Yes."

The next 4 words are as used when gaining rapport: **"Well, you know how ..."** followed by a fact that they will agree with. So for example, "Well, you know how we look after your money?" Or, "Well, you know how I am your Advisor?" This is to get another "Yes" tag and mental agreement.

The next 4 words are: **"I've just found out ..."** This is what I call a brain freeze. These 4 words, whenever they are used, trigger a program in the sub-conscious mind which says, "I'd better listen, because this could be important." This could be followed up with, for example: "I've just found out, you are due for a review..." and a fact about their policies, or "I've just found out there has been a change in the market and we need to run through the updates."

The 5 words are **"Would it be OK if..."** Whenever these 5 words are used in this order, it sets off a program in the sub-conscious mind, and the next word people use mentally is: "Yes," and they say it. So this is easy for a close. For example, you could say: "Would it be OK if we met to discuss this?"

The body of every call is the same; the only slight variation will be the beginning, depending on your relationship with the prospect/client.

Ring, ring.

Bernie: "Hi, is this John Smith?"

John: "Yes."

Bernie: "This is xxxx from xxxx. Is this a good time for you?" – 7 words

"John, you are probably wondering why I am calling." - 9 words

"Well, you know how … (State a fact that they will agree with to build trust.)" – 4 words

"I've just found out … (Statement that gets their attention.)" – 4 words

"Would it be OK if we meet to discuss this in more detail?" – 5 words

Telephone Success Call Sheet

Date: _____

Name	Company	Email	Business	Tel	Appointment ✓	Missed x	Follow Up x	Remarks
				Totals:		Total Time		mins

Ratios: No of Calls/Appointments
No of Calls/No Contacts
No of Calls/Miss

Points to ponder

1. The goal for an appointment, is an appointment, less is more.

2. Match pace and volume of the client.

3. Keep records of phone call ratios; you cannot break records if you do not keep records.

"Success occurs when opportunity meets preparation."

~ Zig Ziglar ~

5. 15 Magic Words

Welcome to the 15 Magic Words Pro-active Agenda Programme.

This chapter describes a simple, tested system that has helped many people gain new clients in almost every meeting where it has been used.

Not only is this a benefit to you and your company but also to future clients. The use of the 15 Magic Words Pro-active Agenda will separate you from your competition. You will gain immediate rapport, credibility and the attention of everyone at the meeting.

Here are 6 of the incredible benefits. You will:

* Look more professional
* Keep the meeting on track
* Bring the sale to a smooth conclusion
* Understand who has the buying power
* Increase your conversion rates
* Be organised and respectful of your client's time

As well as giving you these 6 powerful advantages, it also opens your client's mind so they too buy into this process.

The following is a template for the 15 Magic Words Pro-active Agenda:

5.1. Pro-active Agenda Example

Client company name

Client name:

Your name:

Date:

Venue:

Agenda:

"Accelerating Your Growth!"

1	Client's background	
2	Current position	
3	Possible Challenges	
4	Possible Solutions	
5	Cost implications	
6	The next steps	

This can be used in business-to-business meetings as well as between businesses and consumers. So let's see how we use this programme. Let's assume you have already made the appointment.

You arrive at your prospect's office; maybe you are offered a coffee and a seat.

When you speak to people, you must understand the importance of "rhythms of three." These are three benefits that you offer. They must be totally client-benefit focused; such as more clients, higher profits. You introduce this early to take the meeting away from the coffee and politely prepare for the magic words.

Let me give you an example of what to say before the magic words. This will help you reconfirm the amount of time allocated to the meeting.

"So Dawn, from my understanding, we have 45 minutes to discuss how we can help you get more clients, with bigger accounts and promote brand awareness; is this about right?" (Then pause.)

Whoever mumbles, crumbles. The only answer you should get in this instance is "Yes," as it is impossible to say "No" because it is what they want to talk about. Also, these are blind bullets which apply in their profession. I know what you are thinking now – what is a blind bullet? Blind bullets are general client benefits; for example, my programme will help you get more clients, more easily and more often.

These benefits do not give specific outcomes, but they are general benefits to the client.

Another example would be this: let's say you are meeting a graphics designer.

"So Paul, from my understanding, we have about 40 minutes to discuss how we can help you get more clients, reduce advertising costs and increase sales to existing clients; is that about right?" (Then pause.)

5.2 How to Use the 15 Magic Words

Assuming they said "Yes," you have now prepared them to receive the 15 Magic Words Pro-active Agenda.

So here goes; here are the 15 magic words to set the scene. There are reasons for choosing this particular order of words:

"So... Here is our agenda. Is there anything you wish to add or is this OK?" (Pass a copy of the agenda to the client.)

Whoever hears these 15 magic words will be thinking: "Wow, this person is organised and considerate." They will appreciate this opening.

This definitely separates you from the competition. Now let's break these 15 magic words into groups.

5.3 The 15 Magic Words in Detail

Stage one: The word "So" introduces the 15 magic words and is powerful in this context; it means you have something important to say. If you use the word "So" together with their name, as in "So, John" (then pause), it means that what you have to say is important and it is personal because you have used their name.

Stage two: The first group of the 15 magic words - "Here is our agenda." This politely tells your client that you have been thinking about them, you have prepared for the meeting, and you take them seriously.

Stage three: "Is there anything you wish to add?" This tells your client that, even though you have effectively taken control of the meeting, you are flexible enough to have given them an opportunity to add something. You are not attempting to appear as if you control the meeting completely; you are open to their suggestions. This also forces people to read the total agenda; again, it is a win-win position. You are opening their minds to make it easier to talk about your agenda. This is why we leave two rows blank at the bottom of the agenda for them to add anything they wish.

Stage four: Next, you give them the option to say "Yes" by saying: "or is this OK?" This gives you permission to continue with the agenda. It is important that you pause after "or is this OK?" Again, after this pause, whoever mumbles, crumbles. Be patient and wait for the "yes."

I have found over the years in direct sales with consumers and in business-to-business meetings that, in almost every case, the client says "Yes" and we move on.

Let's look in detail at the 15 Magic Words Pro-active Agenda:

1. Confirm the time allocated for the meeting.

2. Put the client company name and logo at the top. (Check spelling and colours.)

3. Include one client benefit in the headline. Here's a tip; prepare some client benefit headings in advance, maybe have some with you.

4. Your posture when you hand over the agenda gives it great value. You do this by holding the paper by the corners as if it were an A4 sheet of fine fragile glass. In simple terms, you give the agenda a high value.

5.4 How to Use the Agenda

Let's look at the points on the agenda:

1. Client's Background

This is strong and powerful; it sets the scene for the person using the agenda, not for the client. To an onlooker, the word 'Background' is not completely clear but it is to you. It is the cornerstone to the whole process. Let me explain why. We are talking about the client's background, so this is how we introduce it after they have read and agreed with the agenda.

"So, Claire, what made you get involved in marketing?" Or, "So, John, what made you become a solicitor?"

After you have covered the background and listened to them speak it is important for you to tick box number 1. Once this is ticked, they will want to go through the rest of the agenda. If they do not tick box 1 on their copy of the agenda make sure you tick yours so they can see it. As soon as you tick box 1, you know the meeting will go smoothly, like travelling with the flow down a river.

2. Current Position

This will need to be personalised to your business. You might not use the words "current position" but something that is relevant to the meeting. At box 2, you are gathering as much information as possible about the client and company. You are looking for 2 key indicators:

a) The client's pain

b) The client's potential gain

In simple terms, what is causing the client's pain, what pain are they trying to avoid, and what benefits are they looking for in their business? From my own experience, I believe people are motivated more to avoid or minimise pain than work for the benefits they can gain. For example: avoiding toothache gets more attention than going for a massage.

3. Possible Challenges

Again, personalise this to your particular business and to their personal business or circumstances. It is during this stage that you listen carefully to their problems of pain and needs for gain.

4. Possible Solutions

Again personalise this to your particular business and to their personal business or situation.

5. Cost Implications

This is where you talk about potential costs of the solution by working out the monthly cost of the pain (e.g. where they are losing money) and multiplying by 12; for example, if a company's monthly sales are below budget by £2000, you would say: "In the next year, that will cost you £24,000 in lost revenues. If we can provide a solution costing £6000, you would be £18,000 better off."

At box 4, you can even talk about how your client raises a purchase order because, if your phone call was made correctly when you arranged the meeting, you would know that you are speaking with the decision-maker.

6. The Next Steps

This is the point that you bring the meeting to a conclusion and you agree on the way forward with the client. You may decide if there should be another meeting or, possibly, you could proceed there and then with the business.

Priority Action Planner:

ACTION	WHO?	WHEN?

If the client does not write this down you may need to use your own notes to follow up with a proposal letter.

Well, now you have it. This simple method will help you to plan more effective meetings using the 15 Magic Words Pro-active Agenda to get more clients, more easily and more often (without even selling).

5.5 Guidelines Applicable for Financial Advisors

1. State:

I understand we have XX minutes to discuss how we can help you.

2. Emphasise:

The importance of "rhythms of three." Here are some examples:

* To give you total peace of mind.

* To make sure your money is working for you.

* To help you retire in comfort.

* To help you understand your current policies.

* To ensure compliance with regulations.

* To give you one point of contact 24/7.

Of course these are just examples; tick 3 that you think are relevant and create a few examples for yourself.

Tell them that you have prepared an agenda and **pass** it with both hands.

Ask them if they want to add anything or if it is OK.

3. Story:

Tell a true client story that is relevant to the client's situation.

* Background

Tell me how you came to this point - then listen.

Tell me how you came to be running XX company - then listen.

Tell me what led you up to this point - then listen.

(Tick off this part of the agenda when completed.)

* Current Position

Make the client feel good; do a thorough fact-find.

What has been working well for you lately? - Then listen.

Tell me about some recent successes. - Then listen.

What are the best things in your life at present? - Then listen.

(Tick off this part of the agenda when completed.)

* Possible Challenges

I'm just curious, what keeps you up at night?

* Possible Solutions

Book a second appointment now. Set the date to allow you enough time to research the particular market for the client and prepare relevant data for the next meeting.

* Cost Implications

Explain Advisors' Fees as well as the investments they will make, i.e. pension contributions, etc.

* The Next Steps

Re-confirm the date for the second meeting (to take place after you have collected all the necessary information.)

The Contrast Principle

This powerful sales tool is based on The Goldilocks Principle, which is well-known in sales and marketing; yet when tweaked and described as The Contrast Principle, it instantly makes more sense to the user.

You'll remember the story of Goldilocks and the three bears in the porridge scene. One bowl of porridge was too hot, another was too cold but the third option - it's always the middle option - was just right and the one she chose to eat. Time and time again in marketing, particularly on-line, consumers tend to go for the middle option as their best bet. So here's how the Contrast Principle works.

Offering to Place More Fees into Pension

Let's look at The Contrast Principle at work in a client negotiation discussion around a new level of pension contribution. The sale comes from the client agreeing to an increase in their current monthly contribution.

Rhythm of Three

Let's also use the 'Rhythm of Three' here. There are many ways to open someone's mind and get them to drop their preconceived 'defence barriers.' One method is to offer three options. Two or four (or any other number) never have the dynamic resonance of three.

Sales person: "When you retire, what would you look forward to doing? Going on that dream holiday, spending more quality time with your family, or doing something really big and bold?"

Client: "Definitely that last one. Building a new home overlooking the sea in Portugal."

Sales person: "Wow, that sounds amazing. And for you to achieve this, there's no question that your investment would need to be more like one thousand pounds per calendar month or considerably more if you wanted to build a mansion. Tell me what would be a sensible figure...?"

Now we bring in The Contrast Principle.

Sales person: "...Nine thousand pounds, ninety pounds or nine hundred pounds?"

Once again there are three choices and the middle option is the third one, which is what a client will invariably choose. However, do stop talking once you have presented the three alternatives. As often said in sales, whoever mumbles, crumbles. Simply wait for their considered response.

In choosing the third or middle option, add "That's a good choice, and I agree with you." Of course this also means they have taken ownership of what they deem to be their own judgment and thinking.

There are a small number of clients who may choose the first option - the big figure - and it's important to suggest it could be too much of a commitment and bring the figure down to a safer and more manageable amount, which will underline your concern for them at the same time.

To summarise, The Contrast Principle using The Rhythm of Three are two simple yet highly potent tools that you should use when discussing sums of investment; and, like any tool, lots of practice will ensure it works extraordinarily well for you each and every time you deploy it.

Points to ponder

1. The power of the Rhythms of 3.

2. The close is at the beginning: "Before we get started."

3. The first box ticked will result in igniting the cascade process.

"You can't build a reputation on what you're going to do."

~ Henry Ford ~

6. Closing

In this section, closing gets more attention than it really deserves; but many people who want to get to the point quickly ask me:

"How do you close? Teach me this skill."

The reason for beginning with building trust and learning 'secret languages' is quite simple; once you have built trust and learned the language, closing is almost done!

We have touched on how quickly the human subconscious mind makes a decision.

Even if we make lots of magnificent presentations and yet, repeatedly, the prospects still say "No," how much do we earn? Clearly, we earn nothing!

Therefore, we are in the decision-making business. We're not here for putting on lots of presentations, PowerPoint shows, brochures, debits and credits, flip charts, and all sorts of information. Untrained people believe this is all so vitally necessary for them to close more business.

If people do not make decisions on information, then how do they make decisions?

Advertisers sell by using simple 15-second commercials. This brief time is far too short to provide information. So how do they do it?

If advertisers can make a sale in 15 seconds, then why can't we do the same or similar as skilled professional services experts?

If the decision-making process is based on logic, then why do so many people consistently make such terrible decisions?

If you could do away with all the unnecessary boring facts whilst at the same time being thorough and compliant, would you want to help your prospect make an instant and final decision about their future?

Once they have made a positive decision with you, then you can follow it up with all the appropriate information they want and need. After that you can train them with PowerPoint shows and the rest.

So don't throw away all your information tools just yet! The idea is to provide specific information for a particular purpose.

Now that we understand that decisions are made subconsciously, based upon **programs** that are **already** inside people's minds, it is easy to understand how closing works.

1. Closing affects one of the programs within the prospect's mind and commands it to make an instant decision.

2. It motivates the subconscious mind into action, and it is action that we need.

So, just by saying a few words, prospects have an instant feeling, and an instant decision is made in their mind.

No flip chart, no information, no PowerPoint, no videos … nothing else is required at that time.

I can hear some professionals saying: "Oh no, I have been wasting my time over the years giving more and more information!"

It is better to learn this now than for you to continue the struggle to fulfill your true potential.

Here is an example of the 5 methods of closing (1 being the poorest) that I use:

1. What day is best for you?

2. What will be easier for you?

3. Most and some.

4. Are you OK with…

5. Before I start, I tell a relevant story.

If you are a strong supporter of Manchester United, all I have to say is Manchester City and you have an instant feeling, don't you?

You have already made up your mind that you cannot believe me, you can't trust me, nor will you even listen to me.

Of course, it works the other way too!

In my training programmes, I do this part of the session on closing in the studio, a little slower, giving many examples to back it up.

Let's look at the 5 levels of closing.

1. Use an existing close, which many prospects now expect and are becoming immune to as poor quality.

"So what day is best for you, A or B?" This is an old, untrained low-level close, which people can see and hear coming.

2. "What will be easier for you, business with me or for you to continue to struggle?"

Or: "What will be easier for you, to continue without protection for your family or to complete this simple form today?"

Or: "What would be easier for you, to worry about not having a pension or for you to start one today?"

Once people tell you "Business with you," you simply pause and say: "That's a great idea, I agree with you." And they will buy it and take the credit, and want to get started.

3. "Most People and Some People"

"Most people would like peace of mind knowing they are protected, but some people are happy to take the risk."

This is a very subtle nudge to those people who were pre-programmed as minors that they feel safer with "Most" - as most is more - and "Some" is less, and we all want more!

4. "Are you OK with..." These are 4 powerful words where we are re-trying to get a soft "No" response. For example:

"Are you happy with such a low return on your bank investment?"

"Are you OK with not having a pension?"

"Are you happy having untrained people advising you on your company?"

"Are you OK with hoping your advertising words work?"

"Are you OK with such poor results from your presentations?"

5. "Before we start let me tell you a story about..." Then tell a third-party story. As soon as we use the word "story," our subconscious mind can access this programme from our younger days and remember stories are great to listen to.

Or you could say: "Before we get started, let me tell you about a client of mine…"

Points to ponder

1. Close without closing.

2. The 2 powerful words on influencing without selling: "Most People."

3. The 4 words to induce pain "Are you OK with …..?"

*"No man can become rich without
first enriching others."*

~ Andrew Carnegie ~

7. Referrals

Over the years I have worked with many professionals who struggled to get ongoing high-quality referrals. Many paid for different sources such as advertising, mailing, buying leads or mailing lists, etc.

The challenge with this method is that if any of these sources dries up, so do all your leads, and in turn your business could shut down very quickly. The automatic referral system that I teach has benefited many professionals, and enabled them to overcome the challenges of relying upon any single source of leads. Leads do come at a capture cost.

Benefits of Referrals

* Generally, referrals result in increased business, and therefore profits.

* Existing clients, who give referrals, tend to stay with you.

* The cost of finding new clients is lower than through other methods.

* A referred prospect is more likely to become a client.

* Referrals tend to lead to easier sales than cold calls.

* Marketing costs are less through referrals than other methods of contact.

* The cost of setting up new clients is lower through referrals than through other leads.

* Clients tend to provide referrals only when they are satisfied with the service they receive. Therefore satisfied clients are your aim.

* The conversion rate from prospects to clients tends to be higher through referrals than any other type of lead.

* Any increase in your business also increases your benefits.

The automatic referral system has saved these professionals literally thousands of pounds every year. It will give you thousands of low-cost or no-cost leads. There is no doubt that referrals have the least expensive capture cost ever.

So how do we calculate the acquisition cost?

Example 1

Let's say a company places an advert in a newspaper or magazine that costs £5,000 – and they gained 100 new clients from that advert.

The resulting acquisition cost would be £50 per client.

Advert Cost	£5,000
New Customers	100
Capture Cost	£50

Example 2

Similarly, if a company used direct mail to acquire new clients and ran a mailing campaign of 100,000 pieces and converted the responses into 1,000 clients – that would be a 1% conversion rate.

If the total mailing cost is £70,000, then the capture cost per client would be £70.

Mailing Cost	£70,000
New Customers	1000
Capture Cost	£70

I teach this system of face-to-face requests for referrals as a 3-step plan, something you can remember with practice. The first stage is to ask for testimonials. In the second stage, you ask for referrals. In the third stage, you aim to return every 90 days for further referrals.

Stage 1: the testimonials. The testimonials are part of the process of asking for referrals. Most people are more comfortable giving a written testimonial rather than asking for details of their friends and clients. The testimonial serves two purposes; first, it is good evidence when we approach new clients, or you can include it on your website. Second, it helps our personal self-image when we read what others think and say about us.

How do we get a testimonial? I have created 9 easy questions to ask clients. So let's see how to ask these questions.

The Subconscious Encoding Process

Every time we ask a question … it is answered, although the answer may not always be verbalized.

In the referral script, the use of "Yes" tags enables the person being questioned to find easy answers.

The opening two questions enable them to open the "files" in their mind and extract the required information.

The process of gathering referrals is based on the fact that the client is happy with the product or service provided.

This can be focused in the client's mind by a discussion on the benefits they received from the product or service and the fact that they would, no doubt, wish others they know to enjoy those benefits and advantages.

Included in the benefits when asking for a testimonial or referral are 2 hidden secrets:

1. If anyone is uncomfortable giving you a testimonial or referral, it's an indication of the relationship you have with that person.

2. If somebody does give you a referral, it makes the relationship between you and your client more cohesive; for example, if your client refers you to one of his friends or clients, he is less likely to terminate his relationship with you. Clearly, if he met a friend and discussed you in conversation and he had to say he no longer used your services, it would obviously cause some embarrassment.

So let's go through the 6 questions to ask for a testimonial. Please note that each ends with a question, as we are looking for a response. Wherever possible I also encourage people even to write a template for their client. Firstly, remember to ask them what they like about the product or service provided; this makes it easier when you recommend drafting a template for them.

When is it a good time to ask for a referral, and who should you ask? As financial advisors usually have annual reviews, there are three areas to look at.

1. A testimonial

2. Look through the secret grid (later in this chapter) for opportunities

3. Referrals

Six questions for a testimonial:

1. Are you happy with the service I provided over xx years?

2. What do you like best about the service?

3. I'm just curious, would it be OK if you could help me?

4. I've been asked to speak to one or two of my favourite clients about getting a testimonial and I thought of you; would you be happy to help?

5. To make this easier for you, I can let you see testimonials from other clients I have helped. Would that help you?

6. I can e-mail a template or write the testimonial out for you to check; would that make it easier?

Nine questions for referrals:

1. Are you happy with the job we have done (job description)?

2. I'm just curious, what did you like the most about the product?

3. Is it fair to say you probably know other people who could benefit from this type of information?

4. Just imagine you were in my shoes and you were the Financial Advisor, and you could help other people feel safe and secure; how would that make you feel?

5. Is it fair to say you could probably think of at least two people you could help right now?

6. I'm just curious, who would be the first two people you would want to help and why?

7. Is it fair to say that I could probably help them with financial advice more than you could at this stage?

8. Would it be OK if I helped A and B with xxxx? What would be the best way to speak to them?

9. You will probably want to make him aware that I will call; if you give me the number, I won't call until I hear from you. Is that OK?

The Importance of the Referral Form

Dear XXXX, I think the following people would be interested to receive information regarding your programmes. Please send them details. It's OK to use my name when you write to them.

Mr/Mrs/Miss:		Position:
Address:		
Address:		
Address:		Postcode:
Tel:	Fax:	Email:
Company Name:		
Comments:		

Now, it is also essential to have printed referrals forms, as this systemises the process.

As you can see, the form is extremely simple but gives you and the customer a process to follow.

It also means that if you leave the form with a customer, it can be filled in and returned to you – something that is not likely to happen with just a piece of blank paper.

The Secret Grid

One simple method that you could immediately benefit from is the use of a Secret Grid shown in the diagrams in the next few pages. When you complete it for your business from the information that you already hold in your own records, it will give you a better idea of your overall penetration of products and services by client.

This is a simple process that will increase the average value of orders, help you to block competition and identify other businesses you could work with in partnership. You would also be able to capitalise on the expenditure in sales, marketing and development that you have already committed in your business.

You start with the simple diagram that follows.

1. The numbers on the left hand side represent the names of your clients.

2. The labels across the top of the diagram represent your products and services.

Once you've established your clients and have labelled your full range of products or services, you colour in the meeting square where the client does buy your product or service.

So in the first Secret Grid example, you can see that client "1" already has existing business in Illness Protection and Regular Savings and you have introduced the client to Retirement Planning.

Client "2" has products in Retirement Planning and Lump Sum Investments and so on.

Here's the secret. It's so simple:

The gaps that are left in your Secret Grid, whether that's by territory, by region, or by company, are your opportunities for future business. You've already invested time and money to acquire those clients, you've spent the money to develop or source the products and services – now is the time for you to capitalise on that investment and put the two together.

It's simple, yet so powerful.

Many professionals do not keep careful records of their clients – they can't identify current clients let alone lapsed or ceased clients – so you may have some work to do in "tidying up" your records.

And here's another very important point: you can use the Secret Grid in Business and for Later Life Planning as shown in the second and third diagrams.

THE SECRET GRID

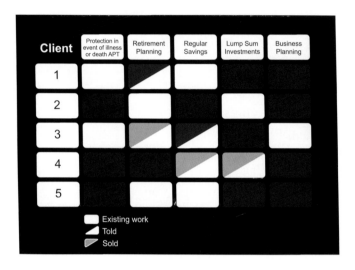

BUSINESS PLANNING

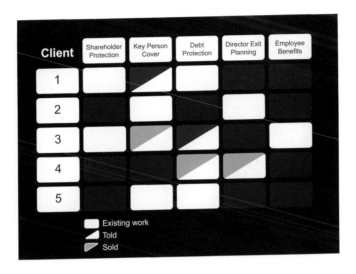

LATER LIFE PLANNING

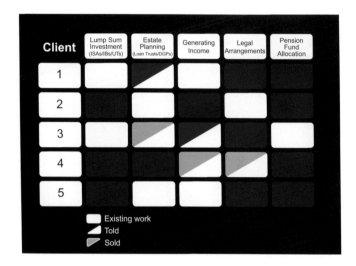

LEGAL

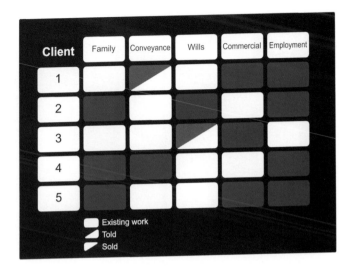

ACCOUNTANCY

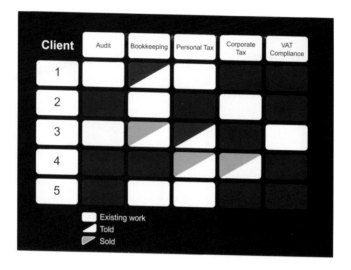

Points to ponder

1. Avoid asking for referrals, most people are not interested in doing this unless you use points 4 and 6 on the 9-step process.

2. An automatic referral process only works once you have proved yourself with the client first.

3. Referral conversion rates are several times quicker than cold enquiries.

*"Self-discipline is the ability to make yourself
do what you should do, when you should do it,
whether you feel like it or not."*

~ Elbert Hubbard ~

8. Time Management

In this programme, I share with you some ideas concerning the age-old problem of time management.

Actually, as we gain more experience, we realise that there is no such thing as time management. However, there is self-management; that is, how we manage ourselves during the 24 hours we have available each day, or 168 hours each week and 52 weeks each year.

How can we benefit from understanding and using these ideas so easily?

Firstly, when we are better at self-management, we become more effective - not just more efficient - in our use of time; i.e. our time management is better.

I'm sure you've heard this expression: "Efficient is doing things right, effective is doing the right things right."

"Efficient is doing things right at the right time."

"Effective is doing the right things right at the right time."

Does your own experience show that to be true?

You find that you:

* Achieve more results day by day.

* Feel far better about what you do, knowing that your efforts are concentrated on the important tasks rather than simply reacting to the urgent ones.

* Have more time available for clients, spotting opportunities to increase sales.

* Create more time proactively retaining clients and generally focusing your efforts on high-return actions.

The result of all these things will:

* Increase your sales.

* Increase your turnover.

* Increase your profits.

* Let you experience whatever personal improvement you benefit from those increases.

* Enable you to have time to achieve your personal and business goals.

When I look at successful people, the top achievers in the business world, those who really are the leaders - I find they use their time brilliantly.

With so much to cover in this programme ... let's get started.

Solutions for Better Time Management

Let's consider some of the solutions for better self-management of time. Let's start by looking at the basics –

we need to understand the problems before we can begin to implement solutions.

1. Value of Time Compared to Value of Task

Now let me give you an example. If you earn £5 per hour and work for 2000 hours your income would be £10,000 per year. I call that in-cost.

The out-cost is what you need to charge a client, at least 5 times the in-cost.

With an out-cost of 5 times the in-cost, or £25 per hour, you will earn £10,000.

If you earn £100,000 per year or £50 per hour in-cost, the out-cost would be £250 per hour.

In some industries the out-cost could be 10 or 20 times the in-cost. For example, to earn £100,000 per year from an in-cost of £50 per hour multiplied 20 times means an out-cost of £1,000 per hour.

Once you have established your 'out-cost' and your 'in-cost,' you know what your real cost is; then you can calculate the cost of any task and ask yourself: "Should I do it, is it worthwhile?"

You can imagine if you had 10 people in a room, with an out-cost of £1,000 each per hour and the meeting lasting 1 hour, that meeting would cost £10,000. Therefore, we need to think very carefully about the value of our time and the value of our tasks.

2. Time Log

My next suggestion for you is to keep a Time Log and again, this is based on the idea that once you recognise a problem, it's easy to find the solution.

A Time Log works like this - on a standard day, you simply divide the day into half-hour intervals on a piece of paper.

As you finish each half hour of activity, you write down on the paper the activities you did. It does take some discipline to do this, but if you can do it you'll be amazed at the information you will find.

You write down what you've done in each half hour segment; at the end of the day - analyse exactly what you have done using three codes: A, B and C.

A - Those activities you really should have done, the main challenges and the main actions.

B - The activities (not the main ones) that you certainly had to do. For instance, in sales, A would be selling time and B would be travelling time.

C - The activities that you know are a waste of time. In other words, you find the actions you take during the day that perhaps you know you really should not do, or that maybe you should delegate to someone else.

If you use more than three analysis points such as A, B, C, D, E, F and G you will find that you simply cannot analyse deeply enough to find the information you need.

You will have so much information that you cannot make any decisions. Therefore, simply stick with A, B, and C, and I urge you to do that as soon as possible.

Once you understand the problem, then you can certainly find some of the solutions.

3. Overview Sheets

I use this idea with a monthly Overview Sheet of my activities, as well as a yearly Overview Sheet. This enables me to take a 'helicopter view' of what's happening in my life, both commercially and socially.

If you don't use Overview Sheets at the moment, I suggest that you definitely start them very soon, to give you a real helicopter view of your life.

Then you can plan things in advance and you can also see how you are spending your time.

Again, a key to so-called time management is to know how you use your time and to be able to see in advance the activities you've planned and to know their priorities.

4. Avoid Victim Language

So many times I hear people using what I call 'Victim Language' - they say things such as:

"He keeps me on the phone for ages."

Now, we need to re-phrase that and say:

"I allow him to keep me on the phone for ages."

"I don't have time to set my goals." That really means: "I don't make time to set my goals."

Therefore, listen carefully to your language. Listen to your colleagues' conversations so you can discern whether or not they are using Victim Language. Then you can point it out to them, and encourage them to change it. At the same time make sure you always use good, assertive language about time management.

5. Saying "NO"

There are times when we say "Yes" and then, on reflection, we think that we really should have said "No."

Have you ever prepared to go out to a party or event and said to your partner:

"I didn't agree to go to this, did you agree? Why don't you call them and say we're not coming?" And your partner says, "No, you phone them and tell them."

Often those occasions can be the times we enjoy more than any other; however, the point is still well-made.

We do need to learn to say "No" more often, and here's a little thought for you that I learned years ago.

Go to your diary or day planner and write the word "No" for every evening in the next three months.

Yes! Put in the word "No" for every evening through the next three months; obviously, this applies to the daytime as well, but you can put it in the evening slot as it doesn't clutter up the page.

This is what you do if somebody calls you and says:

"Can you come to this?"

You look in your diary and you make a decision. If you don't want to go, simply say quite honestly, "I can't make that, there's something in my diary."

The word "No" really reminds you that you have the power to say "No."

I remember some years ago, I lived in the South of the country and I was invited to an event in the Midlands, a round trip of 180 miles each way.

I said "No" because I wanted to spend the time with my family over the weekend.

The person who had invited me was a little upset but that's life.

Sometimes being assertive does upset other people; we don't need to be aggressive, but we certainly don't need to be passive.

So I would suggest saying "No" more often until we get used to saying it.

When we can say "No" nicely without upsetting the other person, then we have certainly understood how to be assertive.

6. Urgent Versus Important

My next idea is that we need to be clear on what the important tasks are that we undertake in our work life and in our social life, and not be tied up every day with just the urgent tasks.

If we are tied up with just the urgent tasks, then the important tasks are left to the end of the day, the end of the week, the end of the month or even the end of the year and are never done at all.

The way for you to know if they are really important or urgent is whether or not you set goals for your personal and commercial life.

When you set goals you know what's important to you, you can prioritise your 'do list' (which I'll cover soon) and make sure that at least part of the day is used for the important tasks as well as the urgent tasks.

7. Clear Desk Policy

You know it's obvious, but: "You need a clear desk." It really does work well and this is why.

Information you receive from your peripheral vision - that's the side of your eyes - impacts you subliminally (below the threshold) and has more emotional content.

If you have ever seen a film on the big screen then seen the same film on a small screen, you know it doesn't have the same emotional impact on a small screen.

Why? Because on a small screen, you see everything in your central vision, whereas on a big screen you pick things up out of the corner of your eyes and that has more emotional content.

In the same way, if you leave information - whether it's reports, files, letters, etc. - on the side of your desk, you will see them out of the corner of your eye and those reports will nag at you, saying: "Remember me, you've got to do me."

You must have a clear desk to enable you to concentrate and to be more effective.

8. Double-Prioritised Do Lists

My next idea for you really is the absolute key to effective self-management of time; it's the Double-Prioritised Do List.

At the start of the day, prepare a list of the actions you plan to take. You may even want to do it the night before, but I do mine at the beginning of each day.

Then, prioritise the list; simply select the top three items and label them one, two and three.

Work on item number one until you can do no more with it even if you have to pass it to somebody else and wait for them to do something. You can then move on.

Before you move onto item number two, re-prioritise the list - in other words review the list and make absolutely certain that item number two has become item number one.

A change in the priorities of the list may be the result of newly received information, letters, phone calls or e-mails or visits by people.

Work through each day taking the actions in order from your re-prioritised list.

At every stage you'll find that you are always working with the highest-priority items, and if you do that, it doesn't matter if some of the actions on the list are simply not done.

Believe me that is the absolute key to effective self-management of your time.

If you stick with a double-prioritised 'do list,' you will find much more work is completed.

9. 1-31 File

The next idea is having what I call a 1-31 File; and this is simply 31 hanging files, labelled 1 to 31, that represent the days of the month.

If I filed something for, let's say, 7th April 2022, then it will be in file number seven.

This is so simple to do. It means you have only 31 places ever to look for a file that you have misplaced.

Of course, with this system, you won't misplace things because you have put them in the appropriate days. I urge you to set up a 1-31 file in a filing cabinet or on your computer for yourself.

Then at the start of each day – simply look in the file for that day to take out the paperwork you've organised.

10. People Files

The next idea is People Files, and this really can save you so much time.

Have a file for each person who is important in your life and - when you think of things you want to discuss with them - put a note in that person's file.

It means that when you have a phone call or meeting with that person you can address all the items in that file and cover them in one session rather than having ten different phone calls or ten different meetings.

11. Establish Uninterrupted Time

You know for yourself there are times when you prepare a report or sales plan or have a creative thought about a client's situation - when you need uninterrupted time.

Therefore, we need effective voice mail systems with our colleagues to ensure that we have uninterrupted time.

12. Telephone Tag

You know what I mean by this. You phone somebody and leave a message, they phone back and leave a message for you, you phone them back and so it goes on.

The best way to avoid this is to have an outgoing message on your voicemail, which asks people to leave the quality and depth of information you need.

Whenever you leave a message for somebody, tell him or her precisely when you called, why you called and what information you need from them when they call you back.

That way if you're not there at least they can leave you the required information and you can cut down on so many opportunities for telephone tag.

13. Completed Staff Work

This works in two ways. Firstly, if you go to a person who has a problem, then I suggest that you have three solutions.

Explain the problem clearly to them, tell them the solutions you've come up with, and see which one they accept. That can save a lot of time.

By the same token, when people come to you with problems, if you've got staff that report to you with problems, teach them to look for solutions in exactly the same way. Very often those closest to the problem are the ones who can work out the best solutions.

Now it may be that the three solutions won't work and you have to suggest another. But it does give you a training opportunity as well.

In time you will find that people stop bringing their problems because they already have the solutions; or they come with a problem but also the solutions and it's easy enough to consider those and say:

"Yes, number two will solve it; do that."

14. Up-To-Date Written Goals

It is essential to have written goals for your commercial life, social life and personal life. This will cover the next year, five years and for the rest of your life.

If you can make the time to sit down and work out where you want to go then it's amazing how effective your actions will be.

Years ago, an old sales manager said to me:

"Bernie, if you don't know where you are going, all the roads lead there." And wasn't he right?

So take the time to set your goals and make them precise - in other words, fill in all the dates and numbers.

Exciting - in other words, you really want to be able to achieve them.

Truthful - you feel you can achieve them because they involve you in effective action and the fact is that you can record your progress along the way. When you arrive, you'll find that you start each day knowing which tasks are important.

You'll know which are the urgent tasks and know precisely which actions to take; and of course, you must allocate time to take action towards those goals.

Allow for thinking time - at work. Think for solutions to the problems that come along.

Plan to avoid problems in the future. I suggest that at the start of each week, you allocate a couple of hours in your diary for that thinking time. In other words, make an appointment for you to think.

15. Delegating

One of the easiest ways to grow a business is to bring people in at the bottom of the organisation who are paid less than those at the top. Then, constantly cascade tasks all the way down the organisation so you always end up doing the things that you do best.

It's great to delegate to people ... if they can: do it faster, enjoy doing it, or do it better than you.

Each day we need to concentrate our actions on those things that we can do better than anyone else, and the only way to do that is to delegate.

You can delegate upwards, sideways or downwards. You can give the task to a colleague, you can give it to the boss or you can give it to somebody who is lower in your organisation. Remember, they must accept it or it may not be done!

16. Know Your Best Time of Day

Personally, I'm a 'morning person,' so I know those early morning hours when the phone isn't ringing are great for working through loads of tasks.

I suggest you think about your various activities during the course of the day and think about activities you've taken in the past.

Do you know what your best time of day is?

If you're a morning person, are you doing your best work at your best time of the day?

And if you're an afternoon person, are you leaving the main tasks until then?

You will find that you do them far better.

17. Handle Each Piece of Paper Only Once

When you pick something up, make sure you deal with it there and then.

I use the Four D's principle:

* Do it.

* Delegate it.

* Dump it.

* Diarize it in the 1-31 file.

Don't use the 1-31 file as a waste paper bin.

18. Avoiding Procrastination

This is my final item for you on the self-management of so-called time management, effective management of time.

Let me tell you a story. Some years ago, a man was fitting some carpets in my house. He was a brilliant carpet-fitter and I asked him:

"Do you ever make a mistake?"

He replied: "No, I don't."

I said: "Surely, sometimes you get it wrong."

He said: "No."

"How do you manage to do this?" I asked.

He replied: "Well, here's how I do it."

"We measure it twice and cut it once, because that way it saves us cutting it twice if we only measure it once."

What a brilliant process that is. You can use this process for avoiding procrastination; here's how you do it:

1. You take a piece of paper and at the top you write yourself a question.

2. "What do I need to do in order to…?"

3. Why ask "What do I need to do?" Because then you've told your mind that you've made a decision to do it.

4. Then you list all the actions you need to take in order to achieve the desired result.

5. On the right hand side of the page, number those items in priority order.

6. Having done that, fold over the right hand side of the piece of paper and re-prioritise the list. In other words, you measure it twice. You then compare those two prioritisations.

7. Then create a third prioritisation, which you know is absolutely the best way to get that job done.

If you do that you'll find you can get through so much more work. That really is avoiding procrastination.

There's a point here: successful people do procrastinate, but they know which items to put off. Make sure that when you put something off, it isn't an important or an urgent task, but it's a low-priority item.

Use the carpet-fitters' technique, as I call it, to measure it twice and cut it once.

Summary

So, there we have it. A vast array of solutions to enable you to maximise the use of your time.

And of course, by so doing, you have more time for the important actions:

* Finding more clients.

* Increasing the average order value.

* Increasing the average order frequency.

* Implementing client retention strategies.

Action Plan

* Work out the value of your time using the formula I've suggested.

* Do the time log - so you know where your time is being spent.

* Start using double-prioritised do lists.

* Put the word "No" in your diary.

* Avoid victim language.

* Establish un-interrupted time.

* Set up your 1-31 files and people files.

* Use the carpet fitter's technique to prioritise the actions you need to take in order to accomplish any goal.

I know that once you implement these strategies and include them in your daily routine until they become habits, you will become more efficient, more effective and achieve more success.

Parkinson's Time Law

A tool that can turn an employee mentality into an entrepreneurial one is Parkinson's Time Law.

So often in work and business, we get into a mental rut and forget that time is much more valuable than money. It incorporates the 'time cheque book idea' that I once heard about. Imagine that apart from a bank cheque book, you also had a time cheque account. When you had to spend some time on something you actually wrote out a cheque in the process. On this basis, how would you now value your time? The chances are, with a completely different perspective. Also think of this as a personal account, whether relating to work or pleasure time. Even though we may be paid for the use of our time, the time purchased is from our personal reserve and can never be replaced, swapped or used on something else ever again - our personal reserve is depleted forever.

The other scary thing is that you do not know the balance of your time cheque account. So by all means you can check how much money you have in your bank account, but where time is concerned, the balance available is a total mystery. No one normally knows the time they have left; yet if you did know you had 50 to 60 years ahead of you, that's very different to only having 2 years left. In the latter situation, the value we would place on each hour left would be very high. Why then do we treat our time supply with contempt? Always thinking along the lines of 'There's plenty of that left,' when we don't really know.

The great thing about Parkinson's Time Law is that it very neatly takes account of these key concepts and packages them into a simple idea:

"Work expands to fill the time available for its completion."

In other words, we stretch out activities to fit a time slot when we don't need to. By doing this, we are wasting our most valuable resource – our time.

Consider an average business meeting in any situation. It's interesting how we pluck an amount of time out of thin air as a 'guesstimate' of what's required. It's usually a rounded amount such as 30 minutes or one hour, for example. Then we proceed to use up all of it and perhaps even more than we planned. That's like walking into a supermarket and saying: "I've got fifty pounds." Then, you go all out to spend all of it regardless of whether or not you actually needed the goods.

Parkinson's Law is hugely important because it helps us in three ways:

* It reminds us time is valuable.

* It reminds us that, potentially, we waste it.

* It reminds us to negotiate with time as a scarce resource.

One way to use the law would typically be as follows: Someone calls you to arrange a one-hour meeting at a specified location. You listen to what the meeting is about and then, rather than putting it in your diary, you ask some or all of these questions:

* Could we possibly do this over the phone or via Skype to save travel time?

* Would it be practical to achieve our outcomes in a shorter time?

* Is there anything we can discuss right now in a few minutes and reduce the agenda?

If you have to meet, being really entrepreneurial, you could say:

* OK, but I won't be able to manage an hour; I'd be happy to make it 45 minutes.

You may be thinking: "Why is saving 15 minutes such a big deal?" Yet think about doing this a few times a week and saving one hour a week. That's 52 hours a year and over 10 years that's nearly 22 days which is quite a chunk of your time. Think about saving several hours a week and what that adds up to over time!

There are so many situations where you can deploy this great time law, yet your main focus of attention should be yourself. Take a long hard look at your diary and prune the time slots you have set up for activities on a regular basis. This means saving personal time resources and having more of it available as a positive consequence.

One frequently asked question is: "This is all very well, but don't you end up working harder and getting more stressed?"

Actually, it depends on your thinking. Saving time doesn't always mean working harder, even though you will of course get more done. Nor does it mean cutting corners and lowering your performance. It certainly does mean that you could invest more saved time for your personal well-being, which is surely worth considering.

Did you know that taking short breaks during your busy day will give you better results than simply getting your head down and going flat-out? This has also been proved many times by runners. Those that stop and walk over a specified distance compared with those that just keep running to get to the end, get further and cover a greater distance with less effort.

Finally, the way to make this really useful time tip work is to remember to use it!

The way to do that is, for the next 3 weeks, have a big note pinned up somewhere or create new 'wallpaper' for your laptop or mobile device.

It's that important ...

Points to ponder

1. Only do what you can do, delegate the rest where possible.

2. Write a list of things you will do the next day before you go to bed.

3. Prioritise the list in importance level, and focus on the task number first; avoid doing what you enjoy doing but do what you need to do.

"Our chief want in life is someone who can make us what we can be."

~ Ralph Waldo Emerson ~

9. Coaching and Mentoring

"When the student is ready the teacher will appear."

~ Buddhist Proverb

"Ability is what you are capable of doing."
"Motivation determines what you do."
"Attitude determines how well you do it."

~ Lou Holtz

Mentoring can apply to an informal relationship between two individuals where one has greater experience and expertise than the other and offers advice and guidance as the trainee proceeds through a learning process.

Mentoring is where an expert allows a learner to observe, follow, and ask questions during real-life working situations. It's a form of on-the-job training where there is little traditional coaching involved. A good mentor is invaluable as you set and develop your personal goals. He or she can lead you round the pitfalls and obstacles that would otherwise keep you from your dream if you were left alone.

At different times in your life, you will have different mentors. You will find people skilled in one particular aspect that you want to develop. They will teach you, help you and guide you round the challenges. You will find their skills are quite different, whether it is physical fitness, finance, computing, relationships, spiritual, or business.

My first ambition was to be a Premier League professional footballer. I knew I could succeed right to the Premier League. Then, at age ten, I shelved the idea. I discovered that I would have to be exceptionally good, much better than I was at the time, to make the grade in the Premier League.

What I didn't understand at that age was that the top players first of all had a burning ambition to succeed in their game. They practised all the hours they could. More than likely they had an excellent mentor or coach. They had someone who believed in them, encouraged and helped them to overcome any obstacles. A mentor is someone who has already succeeded in your chosen field and knows the journey upon which you have embarked. While your ambitions are young in your mind, they are like young plants that need to be fed and nurtured. A good mentor will see potential in you beyond your own vision.

At different times in my life I have had different mentors. I have found that in each aspect of my life, there have been people, skilled in a particular area, who have taught me, helped me and guided me round the pitfalls. Their skills have been quite different, whether they specialised in physical fitness training, finance, computing, personal relationships, spiritual matters, or work.

During my Royal Air Force service, my mentor was also my coach, Bobby Quantock. To me, he was the best instructor of my PTI course at RAF Cosford. When I first joined the Service I was disorganised. I had no dress sense, no routine. The basic training certainly tidied me up and gave me some degree of organisation to my day. Bobby Quantock introduced me to self-discipline and routine in my sports training and also in other aspects of my life.

To me he was a model PT Instructor. He was immaculately dressed and had a great attitude. He was not particularly popular, but I related to him because he was a straight-talker and he focused on results. He helped me to develop discipline and routine. Looking back I realise that, without my time in the Royal Air Force, particularly with Bobby Quantock, I could have easily slipped back into the sloppy habits I had learned from the previous friends I hung around with.

Bobby Quantock was the sort of person with whom I could ask questions on more or less any subject and he would give me wise answers. Throughout my life I have been very fortunate about the people who have helped and influenced my direction at different times.

When we have a clear idea of what we most desire for our future, we set about finding out as much about the subject as we can. We must then go and see, touch and witness whatever is our desire. If we are still convinced it is what we really want, then we need to invest time, effort and possibly money into the subject.

It is utterly pointless to ask somebody for advice if he knows nothing about the subject. All too often we come across people who ask for advice from their friends or acquaintances in the pub. I know this is true because that is just what I did. What we must do is seek out people with experience in our chosen subject or career. This is the time when you learn more about successful people in your chosen field. I remember my school days when I wanted to learn more about top people in sport; at that time, my only source of information was the sports pages in different newspapers.

What Makes a Good Mentor?

It is wise to remember the following points when you look for the correct mentor to help you in your chosen field or any aspect of your life.

* Is he or she where you want to be in this area?

* Is he or she quietly discontented and working to achieve higher levels?

* Does he or she have a coach who is at a higher level?

When I think of the basic qualities required for a mentor to be really effective, first and foremost is honesty. A mentor needs to be honest and demonstrate integrity; someone you can trust, someone who will always do and say what is right in any situation. I felt very strongly that Bobby Quantock was all of this to me.

It is important for the mentor to be competent in their subject. Competence is more than just knowing the subject;

it is also the ability to read a situation, act appropriately and make wise decisions.

The third quality is personality. Choose someone who is results-focused and not process-focused. Your mentor needs to be able to relate well and communicate with other people in the organisation. It is especially important for you and your mentor to understand one another and communicate well, being thoughtful and kind, rather than selfish and self-centred.

Finally, a good mentor has a proven track record in your subject. Ask the mentor to put you in touch with other satisfied clients, businesses or groups of people who they have worked with. If they say client confidentiality prevents them from putting you in touch with anyone and if they have no written testimonials to forward to you, then you should be very wary.

Factors for Successful Coaching

It is worth thinking about where you receive your coaching. If you have a tough time at your office, it is possible that you will have a poor association or mental connection with your colleagues. Therefore, it would be better for you to meet your mentor somewhere neutral. This is likely to be more conducive for success.

It is good for you and your mentor to take separate notes. Your notes would be about what you have learned or discovered, while your mentor's notes would be about what you need to know.

Good times for coaching are early morning from 7am and before lunch. Afternoon sessions are best from 3pm-5pm. You should avoid evening sessions if possible.

In my experience, people who have worked intensely - like many of you reading this book right now - start early and have no real time to rest, so after a challenging day at the office, evening coaching could be less productive.

When is Mentoring Appropriate?

Mentoring isn't necessarily the cure-all and sometimes doesn't fit a particular need. The time when you need a mentor is when you have a genuine desire to step up to the plate in order to make a huge change for the better in your life. Your mentor should always match your passion, drive, energy and commitment. Be prepared to invest in yourself. Because if you are not prepared to do this - why should you expect your coach to put in the effort?

In working environments, mentoring can and does work very well - and is relatively easy to arrange with minimal expense involved.

Types of Coaching

There are various types of business coaching; for example, executive coaching, stretch coaching, team coaches, career coaching and leadership coaching. Coaching is an unregulated business and anyone can set up to coach anything and anybody. This is fine because the proof of the coaching is based on the results that emerge, and if it doesn't work on either side it should be terminated. If the coaching is good, you can expect transformation and results after one single session. This suits certain individuals who simply need a boost or some coaching on very specific skills.

Muhammad Ali and Angelo Dundee

A supreme example of a top sportsman and coach was in the combination of Muhammad Ali and Angelo Dundee. Sometimes we look at extremely successful people and marvel at their confidence. During his boxing career, Muhammad Ali was an example of the best in his sport. We only have to mention his name anywhere in the world and a smile would appear on someone's face because he is universally recognised as one of the greatest sportsmen of all time.

Now who could be a mentor to such a man and give him confidence? Who could encourage him and keep him training? His trainer was Angelo Dundee, a soft-spoken small guy of few words. He was always in the background when Ali was around.

Because of his religious beliefs, Ali decided not to go to war in Vietnam, and he accepted the consequences. I respect his views because he was prepared to give up everything for his own personal views. He served three years in jail, and he gave up the World Heavyweight Championship title, arguably at the peak of his career. Later he returned to fight Joe Frazier for the World Championship.

Ali was under-prepared for the fight, which went to fifteen rounds. In round fifteen Frazier knocked him down a couple of times and went on to win on points. Ali, beaten for the first time in his career, obviously shaken, had to go through preliminary fights again before he had the right to challenge Frazier for the undisputed World Heavyweight Championship.

Their third fight was in July 1975. He called this the "Thriller in Manila." The temperature in the boxing ring was over 100 degrees Fahrenheit, and the fight went to the fourteenth round in which Ali gave Frazier a tremendous punishing. He gave Frazier everything he had in him and thought that he would knock out Frazier, but Frazier was still standing at the end of the round.

Ali went back to his corner and said to Angelo Dundee: "There's absolutely nothing left in me. I know that if I go out there and he hits me once I will be on the floor. Don't let me do this." Angelo Dundee looked him straight in the eyes and slapped him hard across the face. He said to Ali: "You're a wimp. Now stand up." Remember, it was over 100 degrees Fahrenheit in the ring. He made Ali stand up to his full height, ready for the fifteenth round. Ali stood up. Frazier saw him standing there and immediately threw in the towel. Frazier could not go another round. The fact that Angelo Dundee motivated his protégé, when he was at his lowest, when he had absolutely nothing left in him, just to stand up is a great example of how the right mentor can appear at the right time.

In your own work or profession, you will reach a point where you can teach others and share your skills and knowledge. If you have a good mentor, you will duplicate the best aspects of his profession. Remember, and be aware, that any bad habits you have can easily be duplicated.

In any work or profession, first learn, then do and then teach.

I have a saying for myself: "When you're up or motivated you need to go down, and when you are low, or disheartened, go up." In other words, if you are a leader, coach or advisor, when you are at the top of your game, you need to be around people you can help. Conversely, when you are at your lowest, you need to go up to your mentor for inspiration and help.

Points to ponder

1. Every successful individual, company and team has a coach, do you?

2. Find a mentor who has done or helped others to do what you want to achieve.

3. Success is an inside job with external evidence; find a coach/mentor who will give the roots to grow and the wings to fly.

Need more help to get more clients?

Need a speaker or trainer at your next event?

Contact Bernie De Souza at:

Office Phone: +44 1 926 800 163

Email: bernie@berniedesouza.com

If you would like 12 FREE short video clips
on magic word sequences, go to:
www.berniedesouza.com

Other books by Bernie De Souza

Follow Your Dreams

Your Success is Hidden in Your Daily Routine

ABOUT THE AUTHOR

Bernie De Souza has been a professional speaker for over twenty years. He is a sports coach, performance consultant, author and a playing member of the Marylebone Cricket Club (MCC). He has spoken extensively to large audiences in the UK, USA, Europe and Australia.

Bernie first qualified as a physical training instructor and sports coach in the Royal Air Force. Using his experience as a coach and trainer, he is able to provide insights into helping people and companies improve their performance and realise their potential. He has developed an international business through bringing out the best in people. His unique gift in mentoring and personal development has helped many to achieve their goals and dreams. His skill is to make business-building simple.

The information contained in this book will help those who are stuck to become unstuck and those who want to improve their performance to achieve new levels of success.

The message in this book is taken from lessons he learned as he consistently developed his own business. This is not a typical self-help book where you are told what to do. Many success principles are woven into this true-to-life, fast-paced, exciting story.